A City for Ransom

ADULT LEARNER SERIES

A City for Ransom

JUDITH ANDREWS GREEN
DIRECTOR,
ADULT BASIC EDUCATION
MAINE SCHOOL DISTRICT #17

 JAMESTOWN PUBLISHERS

Catalog No. 205

A City for Ransom

Cover Design by Stephen R. Anthony
Cover Illustration and
Story Illustrations by Janet Watt

Printed in the United States of America

5 6 7 8 BW 99 98 97 96

ISBN 0-89061-216-1

Titles in This Series

To all the Greens

To the Reader

Someone was stopping the city. First the subway ... then the bridge ... then the airport .... Soon, no one would dare to go anywhere—anywhere at all.

Suddenly, Betty Rounds found that she and her children were in the middle of it all. Could they get out in time?

Before each chapter of the story, there are words for you to look at and learn. These words are in sentences so you can see how they will be used in the story. After each chapter there are questions for you to answer. These questions will give you an idea of how well you are reading.

Next come lessons that will help you to read, write and spell better. Other lessons tell you things you need to know about, and know how to do, to get along in life.

The answers to all the questions and exercises are in the back of the book. This lets you check your answers to see if they are right.

We hope you will like reading *A City for Ransom* and learning all of the things this book teaches.

Contents

How to Use This Book

1. Learn the Preview Words

Say the words in the box. Then read the sentences. Try to learn the words. See if you know what each sentence means.

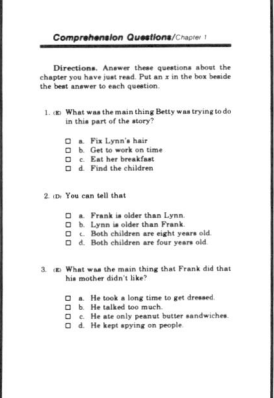

2. Read the Chapter

As you read, try to follow the story and what the people in it are doing. See what happens when the city is attacked.

3. Answer: Comprehension Questions

Put an *x* in the box next to the best answer to each question. Read all ten questions first and answer the easy ones. Then go back and answer the hard ones.

4. Correct Your Answers

Use the Answer Key on page 197. If your answer is wrong, circle that box and put an *x* in the right box.

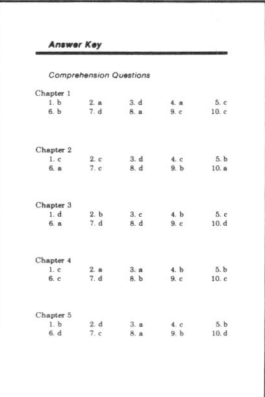

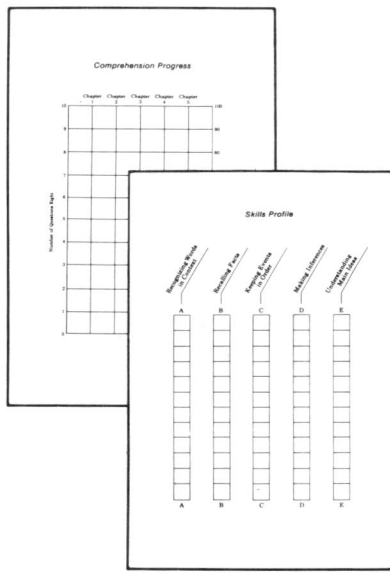

5. Fill in the Graphs

Fill in the graph on page 211 to show your comprehension score. Use the graph on page 213 to chart your skills.

6. Read: Language Skills

This comes after the questions. Read the pages and do the exercises. Use the Answer Key on page 198 to correct the exercises.

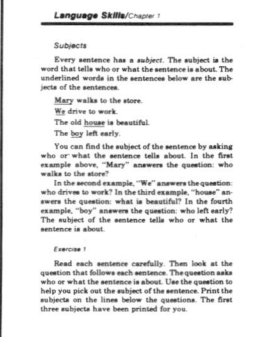

7. Read: Understanding Life Skills

Read these pages and follow the step-by-step lessons. Use the Answer Key on page 202 to check your answers.

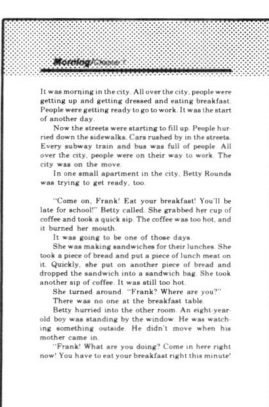

8. Practice: Applying Life Skills

Read the instructions and do the Life Skills exercise. Take your time. Do the work carefully. Try to remember what you just read about understanding life skills. Use the Answer Key on page 203 to correct the exercise.

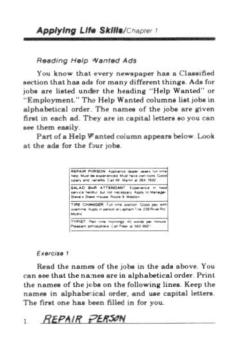

9. Read the Chapter Again

Go back to the story and read it once more. This time, as you read, try to feel all the interest and excitement the writer has built in.

Then, go on to the Preview Words for the next chapter.

1

Morning

Study the words in the box. Then read the sentences below with your teacher. Look carefully at the words with lines under them.

apartment	dangerous	sandwiches	subway
backwards	kittens	shouldn't	suitcases
believe	punish	sidewalks	super
breakfast	refrigerator	somewhere	twenty-four
building	repair	spying	weekend

1. People were getting dressed and eating breakfast.
2. People hurried down the sidewalks.
3. Every subway train and bus was full of people.
4. Betty lived in a small apartment in the city.
5. She was making sandwiches for their lunches.
6. You have to stop spying on people!
7. It was the TV repair truck.
8. You've got your dress on backwards.
9. They had a lot of boxes and some suitcases.
10. Maybe the new people don't believe in beds.
11. It's too dangerous to climb on the fire escape!
12. Please put the milk back in the refrigerator.
13. I'm going to have to punish you for this.
14. The super always gets me a new fuse.
15. Up and down the stairs, all over the building.
16. They shouldn't let kids live in nice places.
17. Fuzz-ball had her kittens. Four of them!
18. Four more cats! She has twenty-four now!
19. I'm going to take the kids somewhere else!
20. The weekend will be here soon.

It was morning in the city. All over the city, people were getting up and getting dressed and eating breakfast. People were getting ready to go to work. It was the start of another day.

Now the streets were starting to fill up. People hurried down the sidewalks. Cars rushed by in the streets. Every subway train and bus was full of people. All over the city, people were on their way to work. The city was on the move.

In one small apartment in the city, Betty Rounds was trying to get ready, too.

"Come on, Frank! Eat your breakfast! You'll be late for school!" Betty called. She grabbed her cup of coffee and took a quick sip. The coffee was too hot, and it burned her mouth.

It was going to be one of those days.

She was making sandwiches for their lunches. She took a piece of bread and put a piece of lunch meat on it. Quickly, she put on another piece of bread and dropped the sandwich into a sandwich bag. She took another sip of coffee. It was still too hot.

She turned around. "Frank? Where are you?"

There was no one at the breakfast table.

Betty hurried into the other room. An eight-year-old boy was standing by the window. He was watching something outside. He didn't move when his mother came in.

"Frank! What are you doing? Come in here right now! You have to eat your breakfast right this minute!

You're going to be late for school! Your sister is all done already, and you haven't even started yet."

The boy held up his hand, but he didn't turn around. "Look, Mom!" he said. "Mrs. Katz is standing on the front steps. She must be waiting for someone. Maybe someone is coming to fix her TV. Her TV has been broken for two days. She has missed all her soap operas. She's going crazy without it."

Betty looked down at her son. "Now, Frank," she said. "How do you know all this? Did Mrs. Katz tell you, or are you making it up?"

"No, Mom, I'm not making it up. I saw her. She watches the soap operas every day. But two days ago, she was reading a book. She never reads books! And last night, she was just sitting there, looking out the window. She almost saw me!"

"Franklin Rounds! Were you peeking in Mrs. Katz's window?"

"Of course I was! I just stand on the front steps and lean way out over the railing. Then I can see right into her apartment. I have to do that! That is the only way I can find out what she's doing. She never comes out. She must be too fat to walk. But look! She's outside today. That's why I want to see what she's up to!"

Betty grabbed Frank's arm and turned him around. "Frank, you must never, never peek in people's windows! Do you hear me? You *have* to stop spying on people! You—"

Just then, they heard a truck pull up in front of the apartment building. Quickly, Frank pulled away from his mother and turned to look out the window. Betty found herself looking too.

Yes, it was the TV repair truck. They could see Mrs. Katz wave her fat arms. She led the repairman into the building.

"All right, Frank," Betty said. "Get in there and eat your breakfast." She looked at a little girl who was sitting on the floor next to the beds. "How are you doing, Lynn?" she asked "Are you getting dressed?"

"Yes, Mama," the little girl said. "I'm almost ready."

"Good girl," Betty said. She hurried back into the kitchen.

She made Frank's sandwich and put it in his lunch box. Then she dropped an apple into the lunch box. She put an apple into her lunch bag, too. Then she put the lunches on the little table by the door. She picked up her cup of coffee and took another sip.

Now it was cold.

Lynn came into the room. Her hair was sticking out all over her head, and she had only one sock on. "Look, Mama, I'm all ready," she said. "I got dressed all by myself."

"That's nice, dear," Betty said. She looked at her little girl and smiled. "Just let me turn your dress around. You've got it on backwards. Where's your other sock?"

"I don't know," Lynn said.

"Well, go back and look for it. OK? And bring me your hair brush."

"But I already brushed my hair! All by myself!"

"Yes, Lynn, I can see you did. You did a nice job. I just want to fix it up a little in back. Now, hurry up." Betty put the coffee pot back on the stove.

"Mom," Frank said, "did you hear about the new people?"

"What new people?"

"They moved into that apartment on the second floor, where the Browns used to live. Right next door to Mr. Logan. No one has lived there for a long time. Ever since the Browns moved out."

"Oh, yes," Betty said. "Are you eating your breakfast?"

"Yes, Mom. Mr. Logan says it's not a very nice apartment. That's why no one has lived there for so long. But these men don't seem to mind."

Betty got another cup of coffee. "Are the new people all men?" she asked.

"Yes. There are three of them. I watched them move in last night. They didn't have much stuff. Just some tables and chairs, and a lot of boxes. And some suitcases. That was all. They didn't even have any beds."

Betty took a careful sip of her coffee. It was too hot again. She put her cup down and went to brush her hair.

"Mom," Frank called after her, "do you think they're going to sleep on the floor?"

"Who?"

"The new people! Those men I was telling you about!"

"Oh. Well, maybe their beds haven't come yet. Maybe they aren't done moving in yet. How would I know? Lynn!" she called. "What's taking you so long? Have you found your other sock yet?"

"I can't find it," Lynn called.

Betty hurried into the other room. "Here it is, right next to your bed. I'll bet you didn't even look for it. Now come and let me fix your hair." She looked at the clock. "Look what time it is! I'm going to be late for work." She hurried back into the kitchen, pulling Lynn by the hand.

"Maybe they got new beds," Frank was saying. "Maybe their new beds haven't come from the store yet. Maybe they got water beds! Wouldn't that be fun? Mom, do you think they got water beds?"

"Who?" Betty asked. "Lynn, dear, *please* stand still. How can I fix your hair if you keep moving around?"

"Those men," Frank said. "The new people. Maybe they don't believe in beds. Maybe they think it's better to sleep on the floor. What do you think, Mom? Do you think they don't believe in beds?"

"Who?"

"Those new *men*! Mom, didn't you hear me? You never hear anything I say!"

"Of course I heard you," Betty said. "Are you done with your breakfast? Good. Get your coat on. Lynn, where are your shoes?"

"I don't know," Lynn said.

"Oh, no! I've got to get to that subway! Look, here they are. Frank, will you tie your sister's shoes for her? I have to pick up the breakfast dishes."

"What do *you* think?" Frank asked Lynn as he tied her shoes. "Are those men going to get beds or not? How can I find out?"

Lynn looked up at her brother. She thought hard for a minute. "You could watch their door," she said.

"But what if their beds come while I'm at school? How would I know? Their apartment is on the second floor, so I can't look into their windows."

"You could get out on the fire escape," Lynn said.

"That's right! If I could get into Mr. Logan's apartment, then I could get on the fire escape, and—"

"The fire escape!" Betty yelled. "You stay off that fire escape! It's too dangerous to climb around on that thing! And you leave those new people alone! I don't want to hear about you spying on them! Not them or anyone else! Do you hear me?"

"Yes, Mom." Frank stood up and smiled at his sister. "I'll think of something," he told Lynn. "I'll find out about those beds somehow."

"Who *cares* about those beds?" Betty asked. "You leave those men *alone*!"

"Maybe she does hear what I say," Frank said to himself. "But only when I don't want her to hear me!"

"That's enough out of you," Betty said. "Please

put the milk back in the refrigerator. I've got to make the beds." She hurried into the other room.

She heard the refrigerator door open, then shut. Then she could hear Frank talking quietly to Lynn. Then the apartment door opened quietly. What was that boy up to now?

Quickly, she made the beds. She grabbed her coat and hurried into the kitchen. Both the children were gone.

She looked out into the hall. Lynn was standing by the stairs, looking down. She could hear Frank running down the stairs. "Lynn! What are you doing out there?" Betty called.

Lynn turned around. She had an egg in her hand.

Betty ran out into the hall. "Lynn! Why are you standing there with that egg?"

"Frank told me to. He told me to wait till he gets down to the bottom of the stairs. Then, when he's ready, he wants me to drop the egg over the railing."

"Drop the egg! Over the railing!" For a minute, Betty could hardly talk. Then she leaned over the railing and yelled, "Franklin Rounds! If you know what's good for you, you'll get up here *this minute*!" She grabbed the egg out of Lynn's hand. Then she grabbed Lynn and dragged her back into the apartment.

Frank popped through the door, all out of breath. "Yes, Mom?" he asked. "What do you want?"

Betty tried to stay calm. "I want to know what you and Lynn were doing with this egg."

"What egg?" Frank asked. Betty held it up. "Oh, *that* egg! Well, I just wanted to see how far it would go."

"What?"

"*You* know! When you drop an egg on the floor, it doesn't go very far. It just makes a little splash. So I wanted to see how far it would go if it dropped from the third floor. I'll bet it would make a good splash! But now I'll never find out," he said sadly.

"Not if I can help it!" Betty yelled. "Frank, what am I going to do with you? That was a dangerous thing to try. Someone could have got hurt! And the mess! Who did you think was going to clean it up? And you have to go and do this right now, when we're late already! I'm going to have to punish you for this. I'll have to think about it. When I get home tonight, we'll talk about it. Now—" She looked at the clock. "Oh, no! *Look* how late it is! Get going!" She gave Frank his lunchbox, then hurried the two children out into the hall. She shut the door and locked it. She ran down the hall. The children ran after her.

As they went down the stairs, they could hear people talking below them. It was Mrs. Katz and Mr. Logan. Did they know what Frank was going to do with that egg?

"You blew a fuse?" Mr. Logan was shouting.

"Oh, no, it wasn't *me* that blew the fuse," Mrs. Katz said. "It was the TV repairman. He fixed my TV. Then he plugged it in, and it blew a fuse."

"I'll bet," Mr. Logan growled. "You need a new TV. Or a new TV repairman!"

"Now, now, Mr. Logan. All I need is a new fuse. The super always gets me a new fuse."

"Oh, all right," Mr. Logan said. "But it had better not happen again! I'm too old for this kind of thing! Up and down the stairs, all over the building! All day long! I have to look after everything! Just so the super can take a week off! I don't know why I said I would do this! Next time the super wants a week off, they will just have to get someone else!" He stomped up the stairs to get a new fuse.

"Good morning, Mr. Logan," Betty said as they went by him.

"Good morning, Mr. Logan," Frank said. Lynn just held tightly to her mother's hand.

"What's good about it?" Mr. Logan growled. He stomped by them. They could hear him saying to himself, "Kids! They shouldn't let them live in a place like this! Always making noise...."

"What a grouch!" Frank said.

"Quiet! He'll hear you!" Betty said. "Good morning, Mrs. Katz. How are you this morning?"

"Just fine, thank you. Just as long as I get a new fuse. I just *have* to watch my soap operas, you know. Good morning, children."

"Hello," Lynn said softly. "How are your cats?"

"Oh, they're fine. Fuzz-ball had her kittens. Four of them! Would you like to come see them tonight?"

"Oh, yes," Lynn said.

"I'll see you tonight, then. Have a nice day."

"Good-bye."

Betty and the children went out the front door of the building. A man was coming up the steps. Frank grabbed Betty's arm. "Look, Mom," he said quietly. "That's one of them!"

"One of who?" Betty asked.

"The new people! The men who moved in last night!"

"He didn't look as if he'd been sleeping on the floor," Betty smiled.

"No, he didn't," Frank said. He looked back at the building. He looked at the windows on the second floor. Those two windows went to the men's apartment. Yes, one of their windows was over the fire escape. Frank ran after his mother.

"Four new kittens!" Lynn was saying. "Four little kittens!"

"Four more cats!" Betty said. "How many does that make now?"

"Twenty-four!" Frank said.

"Twenty-four!" Betty said. "No! She *couldn't* have that many cats!"

"Yes, she does," Frank said. "She got a new one last week. A big black one. That made twenty. And with four new kittens, that makes twenty-four."

"OK, OK, I believe you," Betty said.

Soon they were at Frank's school. "All right, dear.

A CITY FOR RANSOM

Do you have your lunch? And your key to the apartment? Good. Now, you be a good boy after school. Don't get into anything. And don't go spying on those men." She gave Frank a hug. He ran up the steps and into the school.

Betty and Lynn hurried down the sidewalk. At the end of the block, they came to Lynn's day care center. Betty opened the door and they went in.

"Good morning, Lynn," the teacher said. "Good morning, Betty. How are you today?"

"Oh, I don't know what to do," Betty said, as she helped Lynn take off her coat. "That boy! I just don't know what to do with him!"

"Good old Frank," the teacher said. "He's quite a boy. I know we had our hands full when we had him here at the day care center."

"Do you know what he did this morning? He was going to have Lynn drop an egg down the stairs! All the way from the third floor! Just to see what kind of a splash it would make! I stopped them just in time. Lynn looks up to him so. She'll do *anything* he says. It's dangerous!"

The teacher smiled. "I don't think that he'd do anything to hurt Lynn," she said.

"But what am I going to do with him? And this spying on people! It's got to stop! But I can't be home when he gets out of school, and there's no one to leave him with. So he runs around by himself, getting into things. Oh, I don't know why I don't just give up. I hate this city! All the noise and dirt! I feel so alone! We've lived in that building for four years, and we don't know anyone! The Browns were nice, but they moved out.

"So there's Mr. Logan—what a grouch! And crazy old Mrs. Katz. Do you know she has twenty-four cats? Isn't that against the law? I don't even know the names of any of the other people in the building. People come and go so fast. Some new people moved in just last night. Three men. I hope they don't make too much noise. I saw one of them today. I didn't like the looks of him. I hate this city! I'm going to take the kids and go somewhere else!"

"Now, now," the teacher said. "You just need some rest. The weekend will be here soon. Only two more days."

"Yes, I know. I'm sorry to go on like this," Betty said. She looked at the clock. "Oh, no! Look at the time! I'll never make it! Lynn, dear, you have a good day. Be a good girl." Betty hugged Lynn, waved at the teacher, and ran out.

She ran the two blocks to the subway. As she hurried down the steps, she saw that she didn't have her lunch bag. And she had never had a minute to drink her coffee.

It was going to be a long day.

Directions. Answer these questions about the chapter you have just read. Put an *x* in the box beside the best answer to each question.

1. (E) What was the main thing Betty was trying to do in this part of the story?

   ☐ a. Fix Lynn's hair
   ☐ b. Get to work on time
   ☐ c. Eat her breakfast
   ☐ d. Find the children

2. (D) You can tell that

   ☐ a. Frank is older than Lynn.
   ☐ b. Lynn is older than Frank.
   ☐ c. Both children are eight years old.
   ☐ d. Both children are four years old.

3. (E) What was the main thing that Frank did that his mother didn't like?

   ☐ a. He took a long time to get dressed.
   ☐ b. He talked too much.
   ☐ c. He ate only peanut butter sandwiches.
   ☐ d. He kept spying on people.

4. (D) Why did Frank want to know if the new men had beds?

   ☐ a. He wanted to know everything about everyone.
   ☐ b. He thought they would get hurt if they slept on the floor.
   ☐ c. He thought that everyone should sleep in a bed.
   ☐ d. He wanted to take their beds out of their apartment.

5. (C) Frank told Lynn to drop the egg

   ☐ a. right away.
   ☐ b. when they left for school.
   ☐ c. when he got down the stairs.
   ☐ d. when she saw the new men.

6. (B) Mrs. Katz wanted Lynn to

   ☐ a. stop making noise.
   ☐ b. come see her new kittens.
   ☐ c. fix her TV.
   ☐ d. stop spying on her.

7. (B) As they were going out of the apartment building, Frank and Betty saw

   ☐ a. Lynn's teacher.
   ☐ b. Lynn.
   ☐ c. the Browns.
   ☐ d. one of the new men.

8. (A) The teacher said, "We had our hands full when we had Frank here at the day care center." What does this mean?

- ☐ a. It was a lot of work to take care of Frank.
- ☐ b. They waved their hands at Frank.
- ☐ c. Frank put too many things into their hands.
- ☐ d. The day care center had too many children.

9. (C) When did Betty remember her lunch?

- ☐ a. When she left the apartment
- ☐ b. When she left Frank at school
- ☐ c. When she got to the subway station
- ☐ d. When she got to work

10. (A) Betty knew that it was going to be a long day. What does this mean?

- ☐ a. The day would be more than twenty-four hours long.
- ☐ b. Betty would have to work late.
- ☐ c. Betty knew that things would not go right for her all day.
- ☐ d. Betty knew that it would be a good day for her.

Skills Used to Answer Questions

A. Recognizing Words in Context   B. Recalling Facts

C. Keeping Events in Order   D. Making Inferences

E. Understanding Main Ideas

Subjects

Every sentence has a *subject*. The subject is the word that tells who or what the sentence is about. The underlined words in the sentences below are the subjects of the sentences.

Mary walks to the store.

We drive to work.

The old house is beautiful.

The boy left early.

You can find the subject of the sentence by asking who or what the sentence tells about. In the first example above, "Mary" answers the question: who walks to the store?

In the second example, "We" answers the question: who drives to work? In the third example, "house" answers the question: what is beautiful? In the fourth example, "boy" answers the question: who left early? The subject of the sentence tells who or what the sentence is about.

Exercise 1

Read each sentence carefully. Then look at the question that follows each sentence. The question asks who or what the sentence is about. Use the question to help you pick out the subject of the sentence. Print the subjects on the lines below the questions. The first three subjects have been printed for you.

1. Sue runs four miles every day.
   (Who runs four miles every day?)

   Sue

2. The red book fell off the table.
   (What fell off the table?)

   book

3. That man never goes to the movies.
   (Who never goes to the movies?)

   man

4. Ellen reads one book every week.
   (Who reads one book every week?)

   _____

5. Your cookies always taste good.
   (What always tastes good?)

   _____

6. They are late for school.
   (Who is late for school?)

   _____

7. The truck was blue and white.
   (What was blue and white?)

   _____

8. The chair is broken.
   (What is broken?)

   _____

9. The flower blew off the table.
   (What blew off the table?)

   _____

10. We will be late for the party.
    (Who will be late for the party?)

    _____

11. After dinner, Ted washes the dishes.
    (Who washes the dishes?)

    _____

12. Before the storm, the sky was very clear.
    (What was very clear?)

    _____

Exercise 2

Underline the word that is the subject in each of the following sentences. Remember that the subject tells who or what the sentence is about. If you have trouble picking out the subject, ask the question: who or what does the action in this sentence? The first two have been done for you.

1. The <u>dog</u> was lying in the grass.

2. The green <u>car</u> looked like new.

3. His shirt was torn.

4. Her bag was full.

5. I always eat at home.

6. We walked slowly past the house.

7. Frank plays basketball on Mondays.

8. Lisa bought new shoes.

9. The window was open.

10. The night was very dark.

11. My aunt works at the airport.

12. The old man sat on the bench.

The Help Wanted Ads

Almost everyone looks for a job at some time. Looking for a job takes time and energy. One good place to look for a job is in the newspaper. Every newspaper has a section called "Classified." The Classified section of the newspaper is where you will find the job ads. You can find the Classified section of the newspaper by looking in the newspaper index. The job ads in a newspaper change often, so you might want to look at the ads every day.

When you find the Classified section of the newspaper, you will see ads for many different things. You can find the job ads under the heading "Help Wanted" or "Employment." Part of a Help Wanted column is shown below.

Help Wanted

ALARM INSTALLER: Experience needed. Good chance to get ahead. Good benefits. Call 943-1221 or 943-0112.

ASSEMBLY PERSON: Full-time or part-time. Must be handy with tools. Call 837-5605. Ask for Kyle.

BOOKKEEPER: Experience helpful but not necessary. Apply Peerless Company, Route 2, South Adams.

BOOKKEEPER: Part-time. Need experience. Salary based on experience. Jonesville area. Mail application to Box B-178, Times office.

CASHIER: Full-time. Will train. Good working conditions. Apply in person to Lynndale Restaurant, Watertown.

The first words in every job ad tell you the name of the job. The name is printed in big letters so you can see it right away.

1. Look at the Help Wanted column. What job is listed the most often? Print the name on the line below, using all capital letters.

_____

There is a quick way to check all the job ads each day. Just read all the names of the jobs. Use a pen or pencil to circle the name of any job you might be interested in. After you finish the whole list of jobs, go back to the ads you have marked. Read these ads more carefully.

Alphabetical Order

You can see from the Help Wanted ads that the jobs are listed in alphabetical order. That means that the jobs are placed in order according to the letter of the alphabet they begin with. For example, you can see that the jobs that begin with *A* are at the beginning of the list. The jobs that begin with *B* come next, and so on. The alphabetical order makes it easier for you to find what you are looking for.

2. In the Help Wanted column at left, which job is listed first: BOOKKEEPER or CASHIER? Print your answer on the line below, using all capital letters for the job name.

_____

3. If the Help Wanted column continued, it would have jobs beginning with letters at the end of the alphabet. Which of these two jobs would be listed first in the longer column: SALES PERSON or MECHANIC? Print your answer on the line below, using all capital letters for the job name.

_____

Job Titles

Some jobs have more than one title or name. That means you can find these jobs in more than one place in the Help Wanted column. Suppose you were looking for an office job. You might find ads for office jobs by looking for the titles CLERK or OFFICE HELP or FILING or TYPING.

You might find a job in a hospital by looking for the titles ORDERLY or NURSE'S AIDE or HOSPITAL STAFF. A job in a factory might be called ASSEMBLY LINE OPERATOR or FACTORY HELP or NIGHT SHIFT.

You should always look in more than one place in the Help Wanted section. Try to think of all the different names for the kind of job you want.

Reading Help Wanted Ads

You know that every newspaper has a Classified section that has ads for many different things. Ads for jobs are listed under the heading "Help Wanted" or "Employment." The Help Wanted columns list jobs in alphabetical order. The names of the jobs are given first in each ad. They are in capital letters so you can see them easily.

Part of a Help Wanted column appears below. Look at the ads for the four jobs.

REPAIR PERSON: Appliance dealer seeks full time help. Must be experienced. Must have own tools. Good salary and benefits. Call Mr. Martin at 264-7602.

SALAD BAR ATTENDANT: Experience in food service helpful, but not necessary. Apply to Manager, Steve's Steak House, Route 9, Weston.

TIRE CHANGER: Full time position. Good pay with overtime. Apply in person at Lapham Tire, 226 River Rd., Mystic.

TYPIST: Part time mornings. 45 words per minute. Pleasant atmosphere. Call Peter at 563-9021.

Exercise 1

Read the names of the jobs in the ads above. You can see that the names are in alphabetical order. Print the names of the jobs on the following lines. Keep the names in alphabetical order, and use capital letters. The first one has been filled in for you.

1. *REPAIR PERSON*

2. _____

3. _____

4. _____

Exercise 2

Look again at the job ads in the Help Wanted column. Then read the list of places given below. For each place, pick the job that would let you work there. Print the name of the job on the line next to the place. Use all capital letters for the names of the jobs. The first job name has been filled in for you.

1. A restaurant: **SALAD BAR ATTENDANT**

2. An office: _____

3. A garage: _____

4. An appliance store: _____

Exercise 3

Look at the jobs listed below. Two of these jobs would help you learn to be a cook. Print the names of these two jobs, using all capital letters. Your answers may be in any order.

BAKER'S ASSISTANT   SALESPERSON
  COOK'S HELPER   STOCK ROOM CLERK
        ASSEMBLY LINE WORKER

_____   _____

2

Screams in
the Dark

Study the words in the box. Then read the sentences below with your teacher. Look carefully at the words with lines under them.

chariot	footsteps	platform	unlocked
conductor	gasping	roar	voice
emergency	jackets	station	weren't
eyes	jingle	swayed	woman
flashlights	mailbox	tunnel	worried

1. She walked slowly to the 60th Street Station.
2. As she went in, she shut her eyes for a moment.
3. She walked down the subway platform.
4. Betty looked down the long, dark tunnel.
5. She stood next to a fat woman with a shopping bag.
6. With a great roar, the train came down the tunnel.
7. The train rocked and swayed.
8. The boys had on green jackets that said DUKES.
9. Even the emergency lights were out!
10. Where is the conductor? Who's running this train?
11. Suddenly, one voice came over all the others.
12. Someone sang, "Swing low, sweet chariot. . . ."
13. Get them to sing Jingle Bells.
14. It's some men with flashlights!
15. She stopped, gasping for breath.
16. "We weren't in any real danger," the voice said.
17. The tunnel was full of screams and footsteps.
18. I'm just worried about Frank.
19. Don't you ever go near my mailbox again!
20. She unlocked their door.

The day seemed to go on and on. But at last it was time to go home.

Betty walked down the street to the subway. People hurried by her down the steps. Crowds of people were on their way home.

Betty walked slowly. She was tired, and she had so much to do. Ride the subway. Pick up Lynn at the day care center. Walk home. Get supper. Put the children to bed. So much to do. It made her even more tired just to think about it.

She walked slowly down the steps of the 60th Street Station. As she went in, she shut her eyes for a moment. She hated the subway! She hated the noise, and the crowds of people. She hated the dirt. But most of all she hated being under the ground .... Shut in .... Away from the air ....

She walked down the platform, trying not to think about it. A crowd of people was already waiting for the train. More and more people came down the steps.

The train should be coming soon. Betty looked down the long, dark tunnel, but she couldn't see the train.

She looked around. Two men were standing next to her. They were standing with their backs to her, talking. One of them turned around and looked down the tunnel. It was the man she had seen that morning! It was that new man from their apartment building, the one that Frank had pointed to. He was a tall, thin man with long, dark hair. As he looked up the tunnel, his eyes looked mean. Betty didn't like the looks of him at all.

She turned away quickly. She didn't really want the man to know that she lived in his building. She stepped back into the crowd.

She stood next to a fat woman with a big shopping bag in her arms. The bag was so full that a loaf of bread stuck up under the woman's chin. The woman looked tired, too, but she smiled at Betty. Betty smiled back. Then she just stood there and thought about supper. If she got home in time, she would cook that fish she got yesterday.

More and more people came down onto the platform. Then, at last, she heard the train coming. With a great roar, the train came down the tunnel. It pulled up along the platform and stopped. The doors of the cars opened, and a few people got out. Then the people on the platform started to push their way in.

Betty pushed her way into the train with the other people. She stood next to the fat woman with the shopping bag. More and more people pushed in. Betty looked for the man from her apartment building, but she didn't see him. He must have got into another car, she thought.

The doors slid shut. The train started up. Without even thinking about it, Betty reached up and grabbed a strap above her. The train roared down the tunnel.

The train rocked and swayed. The people in the car rocked and swayed. Betty held onto the strap and tried to think about something else.

Suddenly the roar of the train was louder. The door at the end of the car opened. Five or six boys came into the car. They had on green jackets that said DUKES on the back. As the last of the gang came into the car, the door shut in back of him.

The boys pushed their way down the car. They were talking loudly and bumping into people as they came. One of them hit the fat woman's shopping bag. The bread started to fall out, but she pushed it down again with her chin.

Betty watched as the boys pushed by her, one after another. She held onto her purse tightly. But soon they were all by her. She could hear them talking as they pushed on down the car.

Betty hung onto the strap. She shut her eyes. Tomorrow was the last day of the week. The weekend was coming. Two days off with no subway.

Suddenly people were screaming and shouting. "Hey! What happened?" Betty opened her eyes quickly. It was dark! All the lights had gone out. Even the emergency lights were out! All around her, it was pitch dark.

People were starting to move around. They were

pushing into each other. "Hey, watch out!" someone said.

"What happened? What's going on?" Someone screamed, and a little child started to cry.

Now Betty felt the train slowing down. It was stopping! It was stopped dead . . . . In the tunnel. Under the ground . . . .

Betty let go of the strap over her head. She put both her hands up to her face. It was so dark! She shut her eyes to close out the darkness.

"What happened?" people shouted. "Why are we stopped?"

"What happened to all the lights?"

"Where is the conductor? Who's running this train?"

That gang of boys, Betty thought suddenly. The ones in the green jackets. Did they do this? Did they stop the train? They were out there, somewhere, in the dark. Betty felt sick with fear.

Ow! Someone stepped down hard on her foot. The people around her were pushing harder. Suddenly a man shouted, "Hey! Watch out! Who do you think you're pushing? Take that!" He hit someone. Bang! Someone bumped into Betty, and she started to fall. She grabbed for the strap above her, but she missed it. She was going down under their feet! They would step on her! But hands grabbed her in the dark and pulled her up again.

More and more people were shouting. The little child was crying louder. "Mama! Mama!"

"Hey!"

"Don't push! Watch out!"

Suddenly, one voice came over all the others.

Someone was singing. "Swing low, sweet chariot, coming for to carry me home . . . ." The voice was calm and sure. It came from right near Betty. Betty couldn't see her, but she knew that it was the fat woman with the shopping bag. "Swing low, sweet chariot . . . ."

The people in the dark subway car started to calm down. There were a few more pushes and shouts, but they were getting quieter. "That's right," one man said. "That's what we need. A sweet chariot. Not this old subway train."

"Yes," someone else said. "Just get me home."

The song went on. The voice was deep and calm. "I looked over Jordan, and what did I see, coming for to carry me home?" Betty let herself go along with the voice. Another person sang with it, and another. The others just stood quietly in the dark.

The song ended. Everyone was quiet. But somewhere in the dark, people were screaming.

It was the people in the other cars of the train, in front of them and behind them. They were screaming and shouting . . . . All trapped in the dark tunnel . . . . The people around Betty began to move around again.

"We've got to get them to quiet down, too!" someone said. The people in the car stood quietly. What could they do?

"We'll take care of them!" a boy's voice came through the dark. It sounded like one of the gang in green jackets. What were they up to now? "Robert! Benny!" the boy shouted.

"Here!"

"Over here!" other boys called.

"You go to the cars up ahead!" the first boy said.

"Get them to calm down and stay quiet."

"How are we going to do that?" one of the other boys asked.

"Sing to them!" the first boy called out.

"*Sing* to them! But—"

"Get them singing," the first boy said. "Anything. Jingle Bells! Get them to sing Jingle Bells."

The other boys were quiet for a long moment. Then one of them said, "OK, Manny. Anything you say."

"That's right," Manny said. "The rest of you men, come with me. We'll head for the cars in back of us. Hey, lady!" he called to the woman who had been singing. "You're doing a good job. You stay here and keep an eye on the people in this car."

"OK, boys," the woman called out. "Don't think I could move anyway!"

"All right, men. Move out!" the boy named Manny shouted. He started to sing. "Jingle bells, jingle bells . . . ." The other boys started to sing too. Betty could hear them pushing through the crowd, singing as they went. People pushed back to let them through. The doors at both ends of the car opened, then shut.

A moment later, they could hear people in the car in front of them starting to sing. "Jingle bells, jingle bells . . . ." It got louder and louder as more and more people sang along. Now they could hear the people in the car behind them, too. "Oh, what fun it is to ride . . . ." The people around Betty started to sing along. Soon Betty found herself singing too. "Jingle bells, jingle bells, jingle all the way . . . ."

Suddenly, she saw a tiny light. Someone over by the door had lit a match. When it was gone, he lit another, then another. "I've got it!" the man called. "I opened up the emergency door handle. Now we can open the door."

Just then, they could see lights shining around them. Lights were moving all around them on the tunnel walls. "What is it? What's happening?" people shouted.

The people near the windows turned and looked out into the dark tunnel. "It's some men with flashlights! It must be the repair crew!"

"Now we'll get going! We'll get going again soon!" people told each other.

Some of the people opened the windows and called to the men outside. "Hey, man, what's going on?"

"How long are we going to be here?"

"We got the emergency handle open. Should we open the door?"

The men in the repair crew called back to them. "Stay inside!" they called. "Stay inside and wait for help! The third rail is dead. We don't know how long it will take to get the train going again. Just stay quiet and wait for help."

Betty found herself thinking about her supper again. She wished that she knew what time it was. Frank was home all alone. And soon Lynn's day care center would be closing for the night. The train just had to start moving again soon!

The flashlights moved around in the tunnel. Then they moved on. The tunnel was dark again.

And the train was still not moving.

The people in the car began to move around again. They were getting tired of standing up, tired of waiting. It seemed as if they would have to wait all night.

And then, in one moment, it all changed.

Someone said suddenly, "I smell gas!"

"Gas!"

"GAS!"

"Let me out! Get out of my way!"

"Gas! Let me out!"

"Ow! Help! Don't—"

Screams sounded over the shouting as people fell and were stepped on. The crowd in the car pushed toward the doors and windows. Betty was pushed into another woman. But still the crowd pushed and pushed. Betty could feel her breath being pushed out of her.

One door popped open, and then the other. The crowd pushed toward the openings. Screams cut through the dark.

The crowd carried Betty toward one of the doors. She pushed and pushed with the rest of them. She grabbed for the side of the opening and pulled. She pushed through. She was out!

She jumped to the ground. She fell, then got quickly to her feet. Other people jumped down next to her and ran. They were screaming, "Gas! Gas!" Without thinking, Betty turned and ran with them along the side of the train. They ran by the end of the train and kept running. Betty ran with them down the dark tunnel.

Betty's feet bumped over the rails. She bumped into the side of the tunnel. She splashed through cold water. But she kept on running. She had to get out! She had to get to the next station! She had to get out of the tunnel before the gas got to her!

She ran and ran. Her breath dragged in and out. Her chest felt as if it were burning. And still she ran.

At last she could not run another step. She stopped, gasping for breath. She could see other people around her, gasping.

"The gas . . . ." she gasped. "What about the gas?"

"I don't think there was any gas," a voice said near her. "I think it was just that we were all so scared."

Betty looked into the dark, trying to see the man who was talking. "Maybe you're right," she said.

"We weren't in any real danger," the voice said.

"Oh, yes, we were," Betty said. "The danger was us."

Betty stood still in the dark, trying to get her breath. The tunnel was full of the sounds of screams and footsteps, all mixed up. It was a crazy sound. Suddenly, something brushed against Betty's leg. Something soft.

"A rat!" Betty screamed. She was running again, running and running down the tunnel. Every time her foot bumped against something, she screamed again.

Now she could see lights. Men with flashlights were coming toward her. She ran up to them, gasping for breath.

One man reached out to hold her up. "You're OK now, lady," he said. "You're safe now."

Other people came up to them. One of the men with a flashlight turned back to lead the way out. The other men went on to the train.

Betty walked along in the light of the flashlight. She could hardly feel her feet. She was too tired to think.

At last they came to the next station in the tunnel. There were big flashlights everywhere. Crowds of people were standing around, waiting for the train. There were a lot of policemen in the crowd.

As Betty and the others came out of the tunnel, people ran to meet them. They helped them up onto the station platform. Everyone was asking questions. But Betty just pushed by. All she wanted to do was to get out of there. And go home.

She hurried up the stairs. Soon she was out on the street. As she walked the rest of the way to the day care center, she hardly saw what was in front of her. She couldn't feel anything.

At the day care center, only a few lights were on. The teacher was sitting at the window with a few children. As Betty walked in, Lynn ran to her and hugged her.

"Oh, Mama! Where were you?" she asked. "Why were you so late?"

"Where's my mama?" another child asked.

Betty told them that the subway had got stuck. Then she grabbed Lynn's hand and hurried out.

She walked quickly down the sidewalk. Lynn ran along beside her. "What is it, Mama?" she gasped.

"I'm just worried about Frank, dear," Betty said. "It's so late! The poor little thing! He's been alone for so long!"

They came to their apartment building. As they went up the steps, they could hear Mr. Logan shouting. "You— You little brat! If I ever see you near my mailbox again, I'll—I'll skin you alive!"

Betty threw open the door and ran in. Mr. Logan was holding Frank by the arm and waving a letter at him. His face was a dark red. "Mr. Logan! What is it?" Betty asked.

Mr. Logan turned around and looked at her. "Your son robbed my mailbox! He could go to jail for that!"

"Frank! What have you done?" Betty asked.

"Oh, Mom, I didn't rob his mailbox. I was just looking at his mail."

"But why?"

"I just wanted to see who was writing to him. That's all."

"He was spying on me again!" Mr. Logan shouted. "I won't have it! I tell you, I won't have it! When the super gets back, I'm going to get him to throw you out!"

"Mr. Logan, I will punish Frank for this. I tell you, he will never do this again." Betty got Mr. Logan to calm down at last. Then she walked slowly up the stairs. Her children ran up ahead of her.

"Mom," Frank said as she unlocked their door. "You know those men I was telling you about? The men who just moved in. Well, today they moved some stuff *out* of their apartment! It was just some suitcases. But I could tell that they were real heavy. And then—"

"Frank—" Betty began.

"They carried the suitcases down the street. I was just coming home from school. So I went after them."

"Frank! You *have* to stop spying on people!" Betty said.

"The funny thing," Frank went right on, "is that they went to the subway. But they have a car! A little red one."

"Frank, I'm going to have to punish you for this. You just can't go on like this."

"But why would they use the subway if they have a car?"

"Franklin Rounds! Go to bed this minute! You will get no supper tonight! Now go to bed! Go!"

Frank walked slowly out of the room, dragging his feet. Betty threw herself down in a chair and put her head in her hands.

She didn't know why anyone would use the subway if they had a car. Or even if they didn't have a car.

She just knew that she didn't want to use the subway ever again.

Directions. Answer these questions about the chapter you have just read. Put an *x* in the box beside the best answer to each question.

1. (A) Betty <u>didn't like the looks</u> of the man from her apartment building. What does this mean?
   - ☐ a. She thought he looked too thin.
   - ☐ b. She didn't like long hair.
   - ☐ c. He didn't look like someone she would want to know.
   - ☐ d. She didn't like the way he was looking at her.

2. (A) When the subway train started up, Betty grabbed a <u>strap</u> above her. This means she held onto
   - ☐ a. the handle of her purse.
   - ☐ b. a handle of the fat woman's shopping bag.
   - ☐ c. a handle for people standing up on the train.
   - ☐ d. the handle to let people open the emergency door.

3. (E) Why were the people so scared when the subway train stopped?
   - ☐ a. A little child was crying.
   - ☐ b. A man shouted, "Hey! Watch out!"
   - ☐ c. They thought there was a fire.
   - ☐ d. They didn't like being trapped in the dark.

4. (D) Why did the fat woman with the shopping bag start to sing?
   - [ ] a. There was nothing else to do.
   - [ ] b. She just liked to sing.
   - [ ] c. She knew that singing would calm the people down.
   - [ ] d. She knew that singing would make the people cry.

5. (B) What did the boys in the gang do to get people to be quiet?
   - [ ] a. They sang "Swing low, sweet chariot."
   - [ ] b. They sang "Jingle Bells."
   - [ ] c. They shouted, "Quiet!"
   - [ ] d. They turned on the lights.

6. (D) How did Betty's feelings about the boys in the gang change?
   - [ ] a. At first Betty was scared of them, but then she liked them.
   - [ ] b. At first Betty liked them, but then she was mad at them.
   - [ ] c. At first Betty liked them, but then she wouldn't talk to them.
   - [ ] d. At first Betty wanted to go with them, but then she got scared of them.

7. (E) Why did the crowd of people push so hard to get out of the subway train?
   - [ ] a. They couldn't get the doors to open.
   - [ ] b. The repair crew called to them to get out.
   - [ ] c. They thought they smelled gas.
   - [ ] d. The gang of boys was after them.

8. (C) What is the last thing Betty did before leaving the subway station?

- ☐ a. She ran through the cold water.
- ☐ b. She jumped out of the dark subway car.
- ☐ c. She ran away from a rat.
- ☐ d. She climbed up to the next subway platform.

9. (B) Who led Betty to the next station in the tunnel?

- ☐ a. A boy from the gang
- ☐ b. A man with a flashlight
- ☐ c. The woman with the shopping bag
- ☐ d. A police woman

10. (C) When did Betty learn that Frank looked at Mr. Logan's mail?

- ☐ a. When she and Lynn got home
- ☐ b. When Mr. Logan called her at work
- ☐ c. When Frank's teacher told her
- ☐ d. When Mr. Logan called the police

Skills Used to Answer Questions

A. Recognizing Words in Context   B. Recalling Facts

C. Keeping Events in Order   D. Making Inferences

E. Understanding Main Ideas

Action Words

You know that the subject of a sentence is the word that tells who or what the sentence is about. Every sentence also has an *action word.* The action word tells what the subject of the sentence is doing. The underlined words in the sentences below are action words.

Ann <u>swims</u> across the pool.

The man <u>talks</u> loudly on the phone.

The child <u>sees</u> the accident.

Sam quickly <u>turns</u> the dial.

You can find the action word in a sentence by asking what the subject is doing. In the first example above, "swims" tells what Ann is doing.

In the second example, "talks" tells what the man is doing. In the third example, "sees" tells what the child is doing. In the last example, "turns" tells what Sam is doing. Each underlined word names an action. An action word tells what the subject of the sentence is doing.

Exercise 1

Read each sentence carefully. Then look at the question that follows each sentence. The question asks what the subject of the sentence is doing. Use the question to help you pick out the action word in the sentence. Print the action words on the lines after the questions. The first two action words have been printed for you.

1. The boy hit the baseball.
   (What did the boy do?)

   hit

2. The child plays happily outdoors.
   (What does the child do?)

   plays

3. Pat reads aloud to the class.
   (What does Pat do?)

   _____

4. She carries the suitcase upstairs.
   (What does she do?)

   _____

5. The cat runs under the bush.
   (What does the cat do?)

   _____

6. We moved to the new house.
   (What did we do?)

   _____

7. The wind blew the tree down.
   (What did the wind do?)

   _____

8. John drives very slowly.
(What does John do?)

_____

9. They work all day.
(What do they do?)

_____

10. She holds the box carefully.
(What does she do?)

_____

11. Jean swings the bat.
(What does Jean do?)

_____

12. They stole that money from a bank.
(What did they do?)

_____

Exercise 2

Underline the action word in each sentence below. Remember that the action word tells what the subject is doing. If you have trouble picking out the action word, ask the question: what is the subject doing? The first two have been done for you.

1. You <u>hit</u> the nail right on the head.

2. I always <u>see</u> her in the morning.

3. He hears the music.

4. They push the car out of the mud.

5. Joan jumps higher than anyone.

6. Fred cuts the meat.

7. The policeman pulls the child out of the water.

8. The children sit on the floor.

9. We go to the movies once a week.

10. You come to the party, too.

11. Jim throws the paper in the wastebasket.

12. The woman crosses the street.

Understanding a Job Ad

When you read a Help Wanted column, mark the names of the jobs you are most interested in. Then go back and read those ads carefully. The ad below is one you might mark.

> **BARTENDER:** Part-time position, Fri., Sat., Sun. All shifts. Exp. pref. but not req. $6.00 per hr. Apply in person at Colbert's, 150 Carolina Ave., Easton.

1. What is the name of the job this ad is for? You can pick out the name because it is the first word of the ad. Print the name on the line below, using all capital letters.

_____

Shortened Words

You can see that some of the words in the ad have letters left out. The letters are left out to make the words shorter. Look at these words from the ad: "Exp. pref. but not req." The underlined words have letters left out. The whole words are: "Experience preferred but not required."

2. Do you have to have experience to apply for this job? Circle your answer.

Yes   No

You can usually guess what shortened words mean if you know what to expect. You can expect a job ad to say how much experience is needed. When you see "exp." in a job ad, you can guess that it means "experience."

Facts in a Job Ad

A job ad tells many facts in a few words. Every two or three words tell a new fact. When you read a job ad, stop after every two or three words. See if you know what new fact about the job those two or three words tell.

It will be easier for you to read a job ad if you know what to expect. A job ad will usually tell you five facts:

1. pay
2. benefits
3. hours
4. how much experience you need
5. how to apply

The ad below is for a general factory worker. It tells you five different facts about the job in just a few words. Every two or three words tell you a new fact.

> **GENERAL FACTORY WORKER:** Full-time day shift.
> $6.50 per hr. Will train. Good benefits. Apply in person
> at Personnel Office, Thomson Tool Co.

1. This ad tells you <u>how much you will be paid</u>. The ad says you will get "$6.50 per hr." That means that you will be paid $6.50 for every hour you work.

2. The ad tells you that you will get "Good benefits." "<u>Benefits</u>"are what you get besides pay. Some benefits that you usually get with a full-time job are:

   a. a vacation with pay
   b. health insurance

c. a retirement plan that will pay you when you retire

3. The ad tells you the <u>hours</u> you will have to work. It says that this job is for "Full-time day shift."

a. Is this a part-time job? Circle your answer.

Yes   No

b. Would you have to work at night? Circle your answer.

Yes   No

4. This ad tells you <u>how much experience</u> you need for the job. The ad says that you do not need experience. The company will give you time to learn the job after you start. On the line below, print the two words that tell you that you do not need experience. Copy the words exactly as they are in the ad.

_____

5. This ad tells you <u>how to apply</u> for the job. It says that you should "apply in person." "Apply in person" means that you should go right to the company to apply.

a. Print the name of the company you should go to.

_____

b. Print the name of the office you should go to when you get to the company.

_____

Reading a Job Ad

Some words in a job ad have letters left out to make the words shorter. The ad below has four words with letters missing.

> **RECEPTIONIST:** Part-time eves. Must have pleasant tel. voice. Beginning position. Advancement possible. $250 per wk. to start. Benefits Exc. Call Mrs. Jones at 836-9936.

Exercise

Use the job ad to answer these questions.

1. The four words that have been shortened in the ad are given below. Print the whole word that goes with each shortened word. Choose your answers from the word list at the right of the answer lines.

   a. eves. _____   telephone

                                               evenings

   b. tel. _____   required

   c. wk. _____   excellent

                                               week

   d. exc. _____   training

2. Use *whole* words to answer the parts of this question. The first answer has been printed for you.

   a. Print the words that tell you what pay you will get when you start this job.

   $250 per week

b. Print the two words that tell you about the benefits for this job.

_____

c. Print the two words at the beginning of the ad that tell you two facts about the hours you will work.

_____

d. Print the two words that tell you that you do not need much experience to get this job.

_____

e. Print the three words that tell you how to apply for this job.

_____

3

We're Going Down!

Study the words in the box. Then read the sentences below with your teacher. Look carefully at the words with lines under them.

anywhere	dentist	hour	scraped
bomb	dizzy	machine	thousands
breathe	early	newsstand	towers
bridge	forever	remember	twisted
buzzing	headline	rumble	uptown

1. She couldn't move! She couldn't breathe!
2. She was so tired that she felt a little dizzy.
3. But she couldn't stay home forever.
4. I'll be picking you up early today.
5. Don't you remember?
6. The dentist is going to check your teeth.
7. She stopped at a newsstand for a newspaper.
8. The headline stared up at her from the newspaper.
9. The subway train was stopped during rush hour.
10. Thousands of people waited up to five hours.
11. It seemed to take forever to get uptown.
12. The shop was buzzing with talk.
13. She hurried to her sewing machine and sat down.
14. We're going to go over a bridge.
15. See those big towers sticking up?
16. Her legs were twisted up under the seat.
17. A bomb! A bomb went off!
18. Rumble . . . . The sound came from below them.
19. The bus scraped loudly against the railing.
20. You can't go anywhere in the city.

Betty had never been so tired in all her life as she was that night. She went to bed right after supper. But she couldn't sleep.

She kept thinking about all those people trapped in the subway train. Then the pushing, and the running. She could still hear the screams and shouts in her head.

At last she fell asleep. But over and over she dreamed about the subway. She dreamed that it was dark. She couldn't move! She couldn't breathe! Over and over she woke up screaming.

One time she woke up and saw her children looking at her. They looked scared. "Mom? Are you all right?" Frank asked.

"It's all right, dear. I just had a bad dream. Go back to sleep."

But they couldn't get to sleep again. Lynn started to cry. Betty hugged them both tight. Then she got up and made them all some hot milk.

At last the children went to sleep again. Betty sat near their beds, looking out the window. At last it was morning.

And it was time to go to work again.

Maybe she should stay home. After all, she had been up most of the night. She was so tired that she felt a little dizzy. She could call in sick today.

But she couldn't stay home forever. She had to go to work sometime. And it would only get harder. So it might as well be today.

But she would not take the subway.

The children got up and ate their breakfast. They were very quiet. Betty sat with them and drank a cup of coffee. Then she got the lunches ready, and she got the children dressed. All too soon it was time to go.

They walked quietly down the stairs. They went past Mr. Logan's apartment as quietly as they could. Then they hurried down to the first floor and out onto the front steps.

Betty helped Lynn down the steps. She turned around. Now where was Frank? There he was, up on the top step, leaning out over the railing. "Frank!" Betty called. "What are you doing? Get down here right away!"

Frank ran down the steps. "She's watching TV again, with two cats in her lap." Frank said. "Good old Mrs. Katz!"

"I don't know what I'm going to do with you!" Betty told him. "Now come along!" She took Frank's hand and dragged him down the street. When they got to his school, he started to run up the steps. Betty called him back.

Frank hung his head down. "What do you want, Mom?" he asked.

"I just want to hug you," Betty said. "I won't see you for a while."

Frank gave her a hug. "See you tonight, Mom," he said. He ran up the stairs to his school.

Betty went on with Lynn to the day care center. When they got there, Lynn hung on to her. "Mama, I don't want you to go!" she said.

"Don't be silly, dear," Betty said. "You know I have to go to work. But I'll be picking you up early today. Don't you remember? We are going to the dentist to get your teeth checked. Today is your first time to see the dentist! You're such a big girl now!"

Lynn smiled. "Yes, and I'm going to open my mouth wide! You'll see!" She hugged Betty and ran off to tell her friends about the dentist.

Betty walked down the street. It was a few more blocks to the bus stop. But first she wanted to get a newspaper.

She stopped at a newsstand. The big headline stared up at her from the pile of newspapers. THREE PEOPLE KILLED IN STOPPED SUBWAY. "Oh, no!" Betty said. She picked up the top paper from the pile. She paid for it and hurried down the street. Her mind was spinning. Who had been killed? That woman with the shopping bag? Those boys? Who?

There was a long line of people waiting for the bus. "I'm not the only one who doesn't want to ride the subway today," Betty thought.

Betty got in line and opened up her newspaper. She looked again at the big headline: THREE PEOPLE KILLED IN STOPPED SUBWAY. There was a smaller headline under that: CONDUCTORS FOUND TIED UP. What could have happened? She read the story.

> Three people were killed yesterday when their subway train was stopped in the tunnel near 20th Street during rush hour. Many other people were hurt. They fell and were stepped on in the push to get out of the cars. The names of the people who were killed are being held till their families are told.
>
> The subway line was stopped from 4:20 till 9:35 P.M. while the work crews checked the train and rails. Thousands of people waited up to five hours to ride the subway home from work. About 8000 people

were held up or had to find some other way to get home.

Two conductors were found tied up in the train. They said that they had been hit from behind. When they woke up, the train was stopped. They could not tell who had hit them.

One woman waiting at the 60th Street Station said that she saw a man with a gun at about 5:00. She said that he put the gun into a big suitcase. She went to find a policeman, but when they came back to the spot, the man was gone. Two other men who had been standing near him were gone, too.

No one knows how the train was stopped. When work crews checked the rails and the train, everything seemed to be all right.

The story went on and on, but Betty couldn't read any more. Who had been killed? She would never know. She didn't even know the names of the people who had been in the subway car with her.

Betty closed the newspaper. Just then the bus came—and it was already full of people. Only a few more people could get on. The bus pulled out, leaving Betty and a lot of other people standing at the bus stop. "I'm going to be late for work!" Betty thought. But somehow she didn't really care.

Another bus came, and another. At last Betty got on. Slowly, the bus made its way through the crowded streets. It seemed to take forever to get uptown. Betty had never been so glad to see the shop where she worked.

But when she walked through the door, she wished that she had stayed home. The shop was buzzing with talk.

"I didn't get home till almost 10:00!" one woman

was saying. "It took them so long to get the subway trains running again!"

"I know!" another woman said. "They shut down all of the subway line. Even way uptown!" The woman saw Betty come in. "Hey, Betty! You ride the subway, don't you? What time did *you* get home last night?"

"Oh, I don't know," Betty said. "It was late." She hurried to her sewing machine and sat down.

The talk went on behind her. "They still don't know who did it!" the first woman said. "Who do you think got those conductors? What's going on? I know one thing. *I* won't ride the subway again till they find out!"

"I know what you mean!" someone else said.

"You won't get *me* on that subway! Not for a long time!"

The talk went on and on around Betty. But she didn't say a thing. She just went quietly on with her work. She was glad that she was going home early!

At 1:00 she closed up her sewing machine. She grabbed her purse and headed for the door.

"Good luck getting home!" one woman called after her.

"Don't ride the subway!" another yelled.

Betty didn't say anything. She just got out of there as quickly as she could.

The bus ride home went more quickly. "I think I can get used to the bus," Betty thought. "I'll just have to get up sooner in the morning. I'm glad there's a bus stop so near the day care center."

Lynn was waiting for her when she got to the day care center. Soon they were walking to the bus again.

As the bus pulled up at the bus stop, Lynn was still talking about her little friends.

They got on the bus and found seats near the back. The bus trip was a real treat for Lynn. She jumped up and down and talked a mile a minute. She pointed to things she saw out the window.

Betty sat back and watched her. It was good to see her so happy. Betty began to feel better. She could forget about the subway for a while.

"Look, Lynn," she said. "We're going to go over a bridge! We're going to go right over the river."

"In the bus?" Lynn asked.

"That's right. The road goes right over the bridge. When we go over the bridge, look out the window. You'll see the boats on the river."

"I want to see the boats!" Lynn said. She stood up on her seat. "Where's the river? I don't see the water!"

"We're not there yet. Look up in front of us. See those big towers sticking up? Those towers hold the bridge up over the river. They go down into the water, right to the bottom of the river."

The bus stopped at a bus stop. A few people got on. Then it pulled out and moved quickly toward the bridge. The big bridge towers came closer and closer.

"We're almost there! We *are* there! We're on the bridge!" Lynn was jumping up and down on the seat. "Look, Mama! See the water down there! Look—ow!"

A flash of light burned their eyes. Then—BOOM! The sound seemed to bump against them.

The bridge moved.

Crash! The bus tipped over and crashed against the bridge railing. Betty fell, crashing into the seats. Her head bumped hard against the side of the bus.

Other people fell on top of her. Screams cut through the air.

Betty lay still for a moment. Her head was spinning. What had happened? What....

Where was Lynn?

Betty tried to sit up, but she couldn't. Someone was lying across her. Her legs were twisted up under the seat. She couldn't move.

"Lynn! Lynn! Where are you?" Betty called.

Other people were calling out, too. "Help ! Help me!"

"What happened?"

"A bomb! A bomb went off!"

"Look at the bridge! It's all twisted! Someone set off a bomb on the bridge!"

"Help me! Oh, help!"

Betty couldn't hear Lynn. She tried again to sit up. The people on top of her tried to move out of her way. But the bus was tipped over so far that they slid back. Betty tried to crawl up the side of the bus, but there was nothing to hold onto. At last she got her hand around the window lock. She pulled herself up bit by bit. She pushed with her feet till she was out from under the seat. She leaned back against the side of the bus and tried to clear her spinning head. She could hardly see. Where . . . .? Where was Lynn?

Other people were crawling to their feet, holding onto the seats. A man held his hand out to her. She took it and tried to pull him up. He stood part way up, but he cried out in pain and lay back down again. "My leg!" he said. "I think it's broken!"

"I have to find my little girl!" Betty said. She was already crawling over him, up to the other end of the seat. She held onto the next seat and looked all around her. "Lynn! Lynn!" she called. She tried to shout, but the fear took her breath away. "Lynn, where are you?"

"Mama!" a little voice called. It seemed so small and far away. "Mama!" Was that Lynn?

"Lynn, where are you?"

"Under here, Mama! I'm stuck!"

Betty slid down toward the front of the bus. Suddenly a little voice said, "Here I am! Don't step on me!"

Betty looked under the seat near her. There was Lynn, rolled up in a little ball. Betty bent down and touched her face. "Don't be scared, dear. Mama will get you out."

"Here, lady, I'll help," a man said. He leaned against the seat and the side of the bus. He pulled on

Lynn's legs. Betty helped her to slide out. Lynn stood up quickly. Betty threw her arms around her and held her close. "Don't cry, dear," she said. "Everything's all right now. Everything's all right."

"I've got the door open back here!" someone called.

The people crawled along the tipped floor toward the back of the bus. One by one, they climbed down through the open door. Then they crawled along under the side of the bus, where it was leaning against the bridge railing, till they could stand up. Almost everyone was off the bus now.

The bus driver had crawled back to the man with the broken leg. He had got out his first-aid kit. He was tying a cloth around and around the man's leg.

Betty and Lynn were near the open door now. A man climbed out ahead of them. Then he turned around to help Lynn get down. He was holding out his arms for her when—

Rumble.... Rumble.... The sound came from below them—all around them. RUMBLE.

Then suddenly the bridge moved again. The bus scraped along the railing. Betty fell, sliding down toward the front of the bus. The man outside grabbed Lynn, bent down, and ran.

Betty tried to crawl back up to the open door. "You can't go out there now!" the bus driver called. "It's not safe! If the bus goes all the way over.... It would fall on top of you!"

"My little girl!" Betty cried.

"She'll be all right," the bus driver said. "Just wait—"

Rumble.... Rumble.

"The bridge!" someone yelled. "The bridge is

moving! Get off! We've got to get off the bridge! It's going down!"

"Let's move!" The bus driver tied the cloth on the man's leg. "Here, take his hands!"

Betty grabbed the man's hands and pulled. The bus driver pushed and lifted. They slid the man on his back right under the seat. Then they pulled him over to the door. Betty climbed out, then the driver.

The bridge moved again. The bus scraped against the railing. The bus seemed so huge over their heads! They could hear people screaming and running by them. Betty looked through the railing at the river so far below them. "Hurry!" she said quietly.

The bus driver lifted the man out of the bus. "This is going to hurt," he told the man. "But we can't wait." He took the man by one arm, and Betty grabbed the other. They ran, bent over, dragging the man's legs along the ground. The man cried out once. Then he gasped, "Keep going! Run!"

They got out to the end of the bus and stood up. People were running by them from other cars and trucks on the bridge. Some people were carrying children.

Where was Lynn?

"Come on, lady," the bus driver said. Then he called to someone running by. "Hey, you! Give us some help here! This man's hurt!"

People picked up the man's legs, and they ran with him. Rumble .... The bridge rocked a little, and they almost fell. They ran on. At last they were off the bridge.

They laid the man down on the street. Betty stood up and looked at the crowd of people all around her.

How would she find Lynn?

Suddenly she saw her. Someone was holding her up above the crowd. "Mama!" Lynn called and held out her arms.

Betty pushed through the crowd till she got to her. She took her in her arms and held her tight.

Rumble.... The bridge moved again. A shout went up from the crowd. Betty could hear the bus scraping against the railing. Rumble....

Suddenly there was a crash. The bus had tipped all the way over. Other cars and trucks were scraping against each other.

Rumble.... Rumble.... Crash! It was one of the towers that held up the bridge! It broke and fell into the river. The bridge buckled. A car slid over the railing and fell, turning over and over. It hit the water. The other cars and trucks slid, crashing into each other. Two more cars slid over the railing.

The bridge shook and rumbled, but the other towers held. The people in the street were shouting and screaming. Betty held Lynn's face down against her. She turned away from the broken, twisted bridge.

The people around them were shouting and pushing, trying to see. But Betty walked slowly through them, carrying Lynn in her arms.

"Are we going home, Mama?" Lynn asked.

"Yes, dear. We're going home," Betty said.

"But what about the dentist? Aren't we going to the dentist?"

"No, not today. We can't get over the river. No one will be going to that part of the city today."

"Well, we could take the subway," Lynn said.

Betty shook her head. "No. We are not going into

that subway." She looked back at the crowd of people by the bridge. "We're going to go home and stay there. It's getting so that you can't go anywhere in the city. You just don't dare to go anywhere."

They walked all the way home. Betty carried Lynn most of the way. At last they got to the front steps of their building. She was so tired that she could hardly climb up the steps.

As she opened the door, she heard Frank's voice. Then Mr. Logan's. "Oh, no!" she said to herself. "What has Frank done now? I can't stand it!"

But Mr. Logan didn't seem to be upset. "I think you're right," he was saying. "I don't like it one bit. They're up to no good!"

Mr. Logan was talking to Frank and Mrs. Katz. He stopped talking as Betty walked in. He turned quickly to look at her. When he saw who it was, he

came toward her. "I'm glad you're here, Mrs. Rounds. Your son has been telling us about those new men."

Betty leaned back against the mailboxes. "Oh, Frank," she said. "You've been spying again! Right after—"

"No, wait, Mrs. Rounds. Wait till you hear what he's got to say! Now, Mrs. Katz and I were talking about these men—"

"I just don't like the looks of them!" Mrs. Katz broke in. "I don't feel safe with them around!"

"I could hear them talking last night," Mr. Logan went on. "I could hear them through the wall. I couldn't hear what they were saying, but they talked far into the night. I kept having the feeling . . . . Well, I kept feeling that they were up to something. But it was just a feeling."

"But then I saw them, Mom!" Frank said. "They were all out somewhere. Then they all came home, just a little while ago. There's a crack next to the door where you can see in. You can see into the kitchen. When the Browns lived there, I used to watch Mrs. Brown make supper. Anyway, I looked through the crack. I could see the kitchen table. They had big pieces of paper laid out on it. And . . . Mom, they had guns!"

Betty closed her eyes. Why did she have to live in the city? Maybe they *should* move away. She could try to find another job somewhere, and . . . .

"So I thought you would want to know," Mr. Logan was saying. "You had better keep an eye on the children."

"I will. Thank you." Betty went slowly up the stairs, pushing the children in front of her.

She made them a quick supper. Then Frank sat

down to watch TV. Betty got Lynn ready for bed. She was so tired that she felt as if she were walking in her sleep.

She put Lynn to bed. Then she started to go back into the kitchen, but Lynn called to her. Betty sat down on the side of the bed. "What is it, dear?" she asked.

"Mama, that bus .... We don't have to go on the bus again, do we?" Lynn asked.

"No, dear. We don't have to go anywhere."

"Mama, don't go. I'm scared all by myself."

Betty touched Lynn's face softly. "You have to be brave, Lynn, dear," she said. "We all do." And she began to sing, "Swing low, sweet chariot, coming for to carry me home ...."

Directions. Answer these questions about the chapter you have just read. Put an *x* in the box beside the best answer to each question.

1. (B) How did Betty find out that three people had been killed on the subway?

    □ a. Frank told her.
    □ b. The women at the shop told her.
    □ c. Someone on the bus was talking about it.
    □ d. She read about it in the newspaper.

2. (A) When Betty got to work, the shop was <u>buzzing</u> with talk. What does this mean?

    □ a. There was a bee in the shop.
    □ b. A lot of people in the shop were talking.
    □ c. The sewing machines made a lot of noise.
    □ d. There was a funny little noise in the shop.

3. (D) Why didn't Betty talk about the subway with the other women at the shop?

    □ a. She didn't know what they were talking about.
    □ b. She didn't know any of the other women.
    □ c. She was too upset about what had happened.
    □ d. She just liked to do her work.

4. (B) Why did Betty take Lynn on the bus?

    ☐ a. She wanted to give Lynn a treat.

    ☐ b. She had to take Lynn to the dentist.

    ☐ c. She wanted Lynn to see another part of the city.

    ☐ d. She had to take Lynn to the day care center.

5. (C) When did Betty lose sight of Lynn?

    ☐ a. When they were waiting for the bus

    ☐ b. When the bus got crowded

    ☐ c. When the bus tipped over

    ☐ d. When people began running

6. (A) After the bus tipped over, Betty couldn't stand up. She tried to clear her spinning head. What does this mean?

    ☐ a. She tried to stop feeling so dizzy.

    ☐ b. She tried to stand on her head.

    ☐ c. She tried to turn her head.

    ☐ d. She tried to move the things that fell on her head.

7. (E) Why did everyone run to get off the bridge?

    ☐ a. The policeman told them to go away.

    ☐ b. They were all late for work.

    ☐ c. They were scared that they would get hit by cars.

    ☐ d. They were scared that the bridge would fall down.

8. (E) What is the main thing Betty learned about the new men in this chapter?

☐ a. Mrs. Katz didn't like their looks.
☐ b. Mr. Logan heard them talking late at night.
☐ c. Frank was still spying on them.
☐ d. Frank found out that they had guns.

9. (D) Mr. Logan told Betty about the new men because he

☐ a. wanted Betty to ask the men to move.
☐ b. wanted Frank to keep spying on the men.
☐ c. wanted to share his fears with someone.
☐ d. wanted Betty to call the police about the men.

10. (C) When did Betty tell Lynn that she had to be brave?

☐ a. When the bomb went off
☐ b. When the man carried Lynn off the bus
☐ c. When they got to the dentist's office
☐ d. When Betty put Lynn to bed

Skills Used to Answer Questions

A. Recognizing Words in Context   B. Recalling Facts
C. Keeping Events in Order   D. Making Inferences
E. Understanding Main Ideas

Singular and Plural Subjects and Action Words

Singular Subjects

You know that every sentence has a subject. The subject is the word that tells who or what the sentence is about.

Subjects that are just one person, place or thing are called *singular subjects*. The underlined words in the sentences below are all singular subjects.

<u>Pam</u> rides a bicycle to school.

A <u>car</u> needs gas to work.

The south <u>field</u> looks pretty.

In the first example, "Pam" is one person. In the second example, a "car" is one thing. In the third example, a "field" is one place. When the subject of a sentence is just one person, place or thing, it is called *singular*.

Plural Subjects

When the subject is more than one person, place or thing, it is called *plural*. When the subject is plural, it usually ends in *s*. The *s* shows that the subject word names more than one person, place or thing. The underlined words in the sentences below are plural subjects. Notice that each word ends in *s*.

The <u>boats</u> float on the water.

The pine <u>forests</u> were cut down for wood.

The <u>boys</u> helped to clean the yard.

In the first example, more than one boat floats on the water. In the second example, more than one forest was cut down. In the third example, more than one boy helped to clean the yard.

Exercise 1

Look at the pairs of subjects below. One subject of each pair is singular, and one subject is plural. Put an **S** on the line after the subject that is singular. Put a **P** on the line after the subject that is plural. Remember that plural subjects usually end in *s*. The first pair has been done for you.

1. pans _____*P*_____   pan _____*S*_____

2. radio _____   radios _____

3. tables _____   table _____

4. shirt _____   shirts _____

5. keys _____   key _____

6. fence _____   fences _____

Exercise 2

Underline the subjects in the sentences on the next page. On the line below each sentence, print **singular** if the subject is singular. Print **plural** if the subject is plural. The first two have been done for you.

1. The <u>beach</u> was covered with people.

   singular

2. The black <u>clouds</u> filled the sky.

   plural

3. The bridge was washed away in the storm.

   _____

4. John drives a taxi on the weekends.

   _____

5. The apples are in a bowl on the table.

   _____

6. Old newspapers piled up in the corner.

   _____

7. The sheets dried in the sun.

   _____

Singular and Plural Action Words

You know that every sentence has an action word. The action word tells what the subject of the sentence is doing.

Action words can be singular or plural. The action words in the sentences below have been underlined. Look at the singular action words in the first column. Notice how they are different from the plural action words in the second column.

Singular Action Words	Plural Action Words
The bird sings.	The birds sing.
The girl walks.	The girls walk.
The cup breaks.	The cups break.

In the examples above, the singular action words end in s: sings, walks, breaks. The plural action words do not end in s: sing, walk, break.

Exercise 3

Each action word in the first column below is singular. Notice that each word ends in s. Make each action word plural by leaving off the s. Print the plural action word on the lines in the second column. The first two words have been done for you.

Singular Action Words	Plural Action Words
1. paints	*paint*
2. writes	*write*
3. spills	
4. explores	
5. answers	
6. rests	
7. listens	

Exercise 4

Underline the action word in each sentence below. On the blank line below each sentence, print **singular** if the action word is singular. Print **plural** if the action word is plural. The first two have been done for you.

1. Cats usually <u>fight</u> with dogs.

    plural

2. Her mother <u>hangs</u> her coat in the closet.

    singular

3. Mary gives me a glass of water.

    _____

4. The truck stops at the red light.

    _____

5. The leaves change color every fall.

    _____

6. Water splashes all over the floor.

    _____

7. Ron cooks dinner every night.

    _____

Job Requirements

You know that a job ad tells many facts in a few words. An ad usually tells how much pay you will get and what hours you have to work. It tells if there are benefits that go with the job. An ad also tells how much experience you need and how you can apply.

Listing Requirements

An ad will tell you if there are any *requirements* for the job. Requirements are the skills or the school work you need to get the job. The ad below is for someone to take care of apartments. Notice how many skills you need to do this job.

MAINTENANCE PERSON: Responsible person for basic repairs in apartment complex. Must be able to lift 100 pounds. Must have driver's license and good driving record. Must have general electrical knowledge. Good salary and benefits. Call Manager, Shady View Apts., 894-2878.

1. Print the two words that tell the name of this job. Use all capital letters.

_____

It is easy to get confused when you see so many requirements at once. But you need to check if you have all the skills the job requires. It helps to make a list. Put each requirement on a separate line.

To make a list, read the ad slowly. Stop after every two or three words and see if they tell a requirement. Many times, words that tell a requirement begin with the word "must." You know if you see the word "must" that the words tell a requirement. If the words tell a skill you need to have to get the job, print the words on your list.

Look again at the ad for taking care of apartments. A list of the requirements for this job would look like this.

1. basic repairs
2. lift 100 pounds
3. driver's license
4. good driving record
5. general electrical knowledge

Use the list of requirements to answer these two questions. Circle your answers.

2. Do you need to know how to type to get this job?

Yes   No

3. How many pounds do you have to be able to lift?

50 pounds   100 pounds   200 pounds

Read your list of job requirements carefully. See if you can do each thing that the job requires. Print **yes** next to each thing on the list that you can do.

Then print the names of the jobs that you have done that show you have that skill. If you have not had a job that shows that skill, you can use experiences from other parts of your life that show the skill.

A school janitor listed the requirements for the apartment maintenance job. You can see that she used her work and other life experiences to show that she has all the skills the job requires.

1. basic repairs Yes I was a janitor at a school for two years

2. lift 100 pounds Yes

3. driver's license Yes

4. good driving record Yes   no accidents

5. general electrical knowledge Yes I fixed clocks and lights at the school

Checking Job Requirements

You know that a job ad usually tells you the requirements for the job. You should check to see if you have all the skills a job requires.

Read the following ad for a motel desk clerk. Pay attention to the three job requirements mentioned in the ad.

MOTEL DESK CLERK: Must be over 21. Must be used to handling money. Must be able to do business on the phone. Hours vary. Day and night shifts available. Please call Manager to make an appointment, Cranston Lodge, 427-9074.

Exercise 1

Here is a list of requirements for some jobs:

> able to do small repairs
> over 21
> used to handling money
> general knowledge of plumbing
> able to do business on the phone
> experienced with adding machine

Three of the requirements on the list are skills needed for the motel desk clerk's job. Print these requirements in the order that they are given in the ad.

1. a. _____

   b. _____

   c. _____

Look at this description of someone who wants to apply for the motel desk clerk's job. Notice the words that are underlined. They tell you about Jack Orlando's age and skills.

Jack Orlando is <u>24 years old</u>. He has worked as a <u>cashier</u> in a drug store. And he <u>has taken phone orders</u> from customers.

Exercise 2

The requirements for the motel desk clerk's job are listed in the first column. This list gives you the answers to Exercise 1. Check your answers before you go on.

Now look at the underlined words in the description of Jack Orlando. Does he meet all the requirements for the job?

Beside each requirement, print **Yes** if Jack fills the requirement. Print **No** if Jack does not fill the requirement.

Requirements	Yes or No
1. a. over 21	_____
b. used to handling money	_____
c. able to do business on the phone	_____

Exercise 3

The list of requirements for the motel desk clerk job is given again. This time, print the words that tell how Jack Orlando fills each requirement. Use the underlined words in the description.

1. a. over 21

   _____

   b. used to handling money

   _____

   c. able to do business on the phone

   _____

4

A Box Full of Bombs

Study the words in the box. Then read the sentences below with your teacher. Look carefully at the words with lines under them.

address	clothes	heart	Saturday
airport	doorbell	hungry	sleepily
bedroom	doorway	kitty	unroll
busy	downstairs	peekhole	upstairs
cereal	groups	problem	wildly

1. It's Saturday! Go back to bed!
2. I'm not sleepy. I'm hungry.
3. Go get yourself some cereal or something.
4. "Ask Frank," she told Lynn sleepily.
5. She rang the doorbell.
6. He walked quietly toward the bedroom.
7. What seems to be the problem, lady?
8. We're really busy right now.
9. Someone just set off a bomb at the airport.
10. I've got your name and address.
11. She looked through the peekhole in the door.
12. Clean clothes were waiting to be put away.
13. Frank and Lynn sat down in the doorway.
14. It might be one of those groups we hear about.
15. We would have time before they got upstairs.
16. Betty's heart was pounding so hard.
17. He put the maps down and started to unroll them.
18. Downstairs, Mrs. Katz watched out her window.
19. My kitty is out on the street all by herself.
20. She began to pound wildly on the water pipe.

The next morning, Frank woke up early. He jumped out of bed and came over to Betty's bed. "What's for breakfast, Mom?" he asked.

Betty opened one eye. She looked at the clock. "Oh, Frank, it's not even 7:00 yet," she said. "It's Saturday! Go back to bed."

"I'm not sleepy. I'm hungry."

"Go get yourself some cereal or something. Then you can watch TV. But don't wake up your sister. She had a hard night." Betty rolled over and went back to sleep.

She woke up again a little while later. She looked over at Lynn's bed. Lynn was still sound asleep. Betty could hear that the TV was on in the other room. Everything was all right. Almost without knowing it, Betty fell asleep again.

At 8:30 she woke up again. Lynn was standing next to her bed. "I'm hungry, Mama," Lynn said.

Betty lay back in her bed and closed her eyes. She just couldn't seem to get up. Why was she so tired? "Ask Frank to get you some cereal," she told Lynn sleepily.

"Where is Frank?" Lynn asked.

"He's in the kitchen, silly. He's watching TV."

"No, he isn't," Lynn said. "I looked. I can't find him anywhere."

"You can't? You can't find him?" Betty sat up in bed. She was trying to wake up, to get her mind clear. "He isn't in the kitchen? You're sure?"

"Yes, I'm sure. Mama, I'm *hungry*."

But Betty was already out of bed. She grabbed for her robe. "Frank?" she called as she ran into the kitchen. "Frank, where are you?"

There was no one in the kitchen. The TV was on all by itself.

"Frank?" Betty ran to the front door of the apartment. She opened it and looked up and down the hall. No one was there. "Frank?" She ran over to the stairs and called down them. "Frank?"

"Mom? I'm down here!" It was Frank's voice. But he sounded so far away—as if he were inside something! Or behind a door—the apartment door below! He was locked in! Those new men! Those men with the guns had him locked in their apartment!

"Lynn! Stay in the apartment and close the door!" Betty shouted. "Don't let in anyone but me!" Holding her robe around her, Betty ran down the stairs. She

ran down the hall to the men's apartment. She banged on the door, shouting, "Frank! Come out! Oh, let him go! Please let him go!"

Down the hall, another door opened. Frank came out. He stood with his mouth hanging open, watching his mother. "Mom?" he said at last. "Mom, what are you doing?"

Betty's hands hit the door one more time. But she didn't lift them again. She stood leaning against the door, looking down at the floor. At last she said, "Frank, where were you?"

"I was in Mr. Logan's apartment," Frank said. "Where did you think I was? Did you think I was in there? Why? Why would I be in there?"

"Never mind," Betty said. "What were you doing in Mr. Logan's apartment? I thought you were in our kitchen watching TV."

"Well, I *was* watching TV. But then I looked out the window and saw those men. They were putting their big suitcases into their car. Then they came back inside again. I just had to find out what they were up to. I had to move fast, or they would take off before I could find out where they were going. So I hid on the stairs. I could hear what they were saying when they came out again. They were talking about the best way to go."

"Where?" Betty found herself asking. "Where were they going?"

"I don't know for sure. I think it was somewhere outside the city. But not too far away. They were going to take the main road out of the city. But they said they had to be there by 8:00. So they couldn't have gone too far."

"But where?" Betty asked again. "Where were they going? What were they going to do?"

"I don't know," Frank said. "So I went to see Mr. Logan. I thought he might have heard them talking again through the wall."

Betty looked toward Mr. Logan's door. Mr. Logan was standing there, looking at them quietly. Betty pulled her robe more tightly around her, then said, "Good morning."

"Good morning, Mrs. Rounds," Mr. Logan said. "Your son and I have had quite a talk." He walked down the hall to where they were standing and gave Frank a pat on the head. "He sure knows everything about everyone, doesn't he?"

Betty tried to smile. "What about those men?" she asked quickly.

"I don't know. I don't know what they're up to. It may be nothing at all. But . . . . I just don't like it."

"I know, Mom!" Frank said. "I could sneak into their apartment! Mr. Logan has all the keys. Don't you, Mr. Logan? You could let me in. Then I could hide. And I could wait for them to come back. Then I could hear what they say. Then—"

He turned to look at his mother. Betty was staring at him, her eyes wide with fear. "Frank!" she said at last. "Don't you even *think* about doing a thing like that!" She grabbed him by the arm and pulled him toward the stairs. "Good-bye, Mr. Logan," she called back. "Thank you for taking such *good* care of Frank!"

She dragged Frank up the stairs and down the hall to their own door. She tried to open the door. It was locked. Betty banged on the door. She rang the doorbell. But no one came to the door.

"Lynn!" she shouted. "Lynn! It's me! It's Mama! *Open this door!*"

The door opened a little bit. Lynn looked out through the crack. Betty could see that she had been crying.

Betty hurried in and hugged Lynn close. "Lynn, dear, it's all right. Everything is all right now."

Frank came in and closed the door quietly. He walked quietly toward the bedroom.

"Franklin Rounds! Where do you think you're going?" Betty called. "You come back here this minute!" Frank came back and stood in front of her. "What do you have to say for yourself?" Betty asked. "Going out by yourself like that! Spying on those men! *Anything* could have happened! Look at your sister! See how scared she was? How do you think *I* felt when I woke up and you were gone? I didn't know where you were! Anything could have happened! *Anything!* What do you have to say?"

Frank just looked down at the floor. He didn't say anything.

"Well? Can you tell me that this will never happen again?"

Frank didn't move.

Betty grabbed his arm and shook him. "Say it! Tell me that this will never happen again!"

"But, Mom . . ." Frank said. "I just *have* to find out what those men are doing!"

"Go to bed! Right now!" Betty shouted. Frank ran into the bedroom and shut the door.

Betty threw herself into a chair. She put her face in her hands. "What am I going to do?" she cried.

Lynn crawled into her lap. "What is it, Mama?" she asked.

"Oh, I don't know. We've got to get out of this city! We've got to move away from here!"

"Move?" Lynn cried. "Oh, no, Mama! I like it here! I like this apartment! I like my day care center! And next year I'm going to go to Frank's school! You said so! I want to stay here!"

"Yes, but.... I just can't seem to stop Frank. Sooner or later, he's going to run into those men."

"What men, Mama?"

"There are some bad men living right downstairs."

Lynn's eyes got wide. "Oh, bad men!" she said. "Just like on TV! Mama, did you call the police?"

"No, of course not," Betty said. "Wait a minute! Why not? It's the police's job to take care of us." Before she could change her mind, Betty set Lynn down on the floor. She jumped up and ran to the phone.

She called the police. Their phone rang and rang. At last a man's voice said, "Police Station!"

"My name is Betty Rounds. I live at 862 18th Street. I—" Betty couldn't think of what to say next.

"What seems to be the problem, lady?" the policeman asked. "Please try to hurry."

"Well.... There are some new people in our apartment building. Three men.... And.... Well, we just don't like the looks of them, that's all. I have two small children, and—"

"Have they *done* anything? These new people? Have they done anything to you?"

"Well, no. But they do have guns. My son says he saw them."

"I'm sorry," the policeman said. "I can't send someone up to check them out just because a little kid thinks he saw guns. We're really busy right now, and—"

"But .... But .... They're up to something! We just know it! You've *got* to send someone!"

"I'm sorry, lady. We've got our own problems today. Someone just set off a bomb at the airport. A big one. Two planes and a waiting room are gone. We don't even know yet how many people were hurt. But we've had to shut the airport right down. There won't be any planes in or out of there till we find out what's going on.

"So you see, we've had to send every car we could out there. We can't send anyone else out unless it's a real emergency.

"Look, I've got down your name and address. Maybe we'll get some time later today. Or maybe tomorrow. Then I can send someone over to talk to you. You'll be home?"

"Yes, I think so."

"Good. Now I've got some more calls coming in. Have a nice day." The line went dead.

Betty hung up her phone. "*They're* a big help!" she said to herself. She went over to the stove and put on some water for coffee. "Come on, Lynn," she called. "We might as well get dressed."

She was fixing Lynn's hair when the doorbell rang. What now? She went into the kitchen and looked through the peekhole in the door. Mr. Logan was standing outside.

"Come in, Mr. Logan," Betty said as she opened the door. Then she saw that Mrs. Katz was standing there too. "Why, hello, Mrs. Katz! How nice! Won't you come in? I was just making some coffee," Betty said.

She closed the door and turned around. Mr. Logan and Mrs. Katz were standing in the middle of the room. The table was full of dishes and cereal boxes. The chairs were full of clean clothes waiting to be put away. Frank's clothes from the day before were all over the floor.

Betty ran over and grabbed up the clean clothes. She hurried into the bedroom with them. "Frank, get in there and pick up your clothes!" she told her son. She hurried back into the kitchen. "Have a chair," she told Mr. Logan and Mrs. Katz. "I'm sorry everything is such a mess! It's been a long week!" She cleaned off the table and began to make the coffee.

Mr. Logan sat down. "We've been talking some more about those men," he said. "We really feel that something must be done. We came to you because you're the one with children. So we knew that you've been thinking about them, too."

"Yes, I have," Betty said. "But what can we do?"

"We thought that maybe one of us should call the police," Mr. Logan went on. "What do you think?"

"Mama already called the police!" Lynn said.

"You *did*? What did they say?" asked Frank from the floor.

"Be quiet, children," Betty said. "Go into the bedroom, both of you. Frank, take those clothes with you!" Frank and Lynn went into the bedroom, but they sat down in the doorway.

"What *did* the police say?" Mr. Logan asked.

"They were too busy to talk to me. Someone set off a bomb at the airport. They were all out there."

"Wow! A bomb!" Frank said.

"Frank, close that door! Now! Yes, the policeman I talked to was all upset."

"What happened? Were a lot of people hurt?" Mr. Logan asked.

"They didn't know yet. The bomb got two planes on the ground and a waiting room, I think. I can't really remember what he said. Oh, Mrs. Katz, do sit down. Do you take anything in your coffee? Here you are." Betty gave Mrs. Katz a cup of coffee. "The policeman did take my name and address," she went on. "He said they might come later today or tomorrow. But I'm not holding my breath."

"No," Mr. Logan said. "We won't get any help from them."

"Oh, dear," Mrs. Katz said. "What *are* we going to do?"

"Just hope for the best," Mr. Logan said. "When the super gets back next week, I'll talk to him about those men. Till then, all we can do is hope for the best."

"I'm thinking of moving," Betty said. "Getting right out of the city. It's not a safe place for the children. Just look at the last few days! The subway. Then the bridge. Now the airport. Who's behind all this?"

"Oh, dear. Do you think it might be one of those *groups* we hear about?" Mrs. Katz asked. "I hope it isn't those men!"

Mr. Logan put down his coffee cup. "Now, now, Mrs. Katz," he started to say, "I don't think—"

"That's it!" Frank opened the bedroom door and ran in. "It must be them!" he yelled. "I heard what you were saying about the airport and all. It must be them!

You know those big pieces of paper I saw in their apartment? They must be plans! Maps! Maps of the airport and the subway and the streets! And then all those boxes! Bombs! That's what they've got in those boxes!"

"Oh, dear, oh, dear," Mrs. Katz said. "Right here in our own building!"

"No, I don't think those men are up to anything like that," Mr. Logan said. "But we really should find out." He looked at Betty. "We've got to go into that apartment and look."

"Oh, no!" Betty cried. "That wouldn't be safe!"

"I'll do it!" Frank said. "I'll go in! I'll find out!"

"No, you won't!" Betty said. "I don't want to hear anything more about it!" She turned to Mr. Logan. "Now see what you've done!"

"Now, now. I'm sure those men aren't doing anything bad," Mr. Logan said. "Not as bad as that, anyway. I'm sure we wouldn't be in any danger from them. But we really should check them out. They're gone now. I've got a key. We could be in and out again in a minute. Mrs. Katz could watch for them."

"Yes, I could watch out my window," Mrs. Katz said. "I know! If I see them coming, I'll bang on the water pipe. It goes right up through their apartment. I used to call Mrs. Brown that way when she lived there."

"See? If they came, we would still have lots of time to get out before they got upstairs," Mr. Logan said. "But we need two people. Two people could check it out so much faster. I don't move around as well as I used to."

"I'll do it, Mom! Let me do it!" Frank said.

"Shut up!" Betty yelled at him. "You're not going out of this apartment, and that's that!" She turned to Mr. Logan. "I can see that I'll have to do it—just to keep this son of mine from doing it."

"Good!" said Mr. Logan. "Let's go! We can't wait a minute. They might be back any time."

"Thanks a lot!" Betty said.

A few minutes later, they were ready. Mr. Logan had the key to the apartment. Mrs. Katz was standing by her window. She had a spoon in her hand, ready to bang on the water pipe.

Mr. Logan stuck his head in her door. "All set?" he called.

"All set," Mrs. Katz said.

Mr. Logan ran up the stairs. He pounded on the men's door, just to be sure. "Super!" he called. "Super! It's Mr. Logan! I've come to fix the pipe!" He put his ear to the door. "All clear," he told Betty.

He stuck the key in the lock and turned it. He opened the door. He walked quietly in.

Betty's heart was pounding so hard that she thought it could be heard out on the street. But she went in after Mr. Logan.

There was almost nothing in the apartment. A few tables and chairs, and some sleeping bags. That was all.

Betty took a few more steps into the room. Where were the boxes? Did the men take everything with them?

"I'll look in the bedroom," Mr. Logan said. He walked through the doorway. "Yes, here they are," he called. "The boxes are in here." He came back into the kitchen carrying some big maps all rolled up. He put them down on a table by the door and started to unroll them. "I'll look at these," he said. "You go see what's in the other box."

Betty took a few more steps into the room. She looked over toward the window. Was Mrs. Katz watching the street? "Come on! Hurry!" said Mr. Logan.

Betty went into the other room. Two boxes sat in the middle of the floor. One was standing open, with a few rolls of paper left in it. Betty opened the other box.

In the box were rolls of wire, and some little boxes, and... little bags that said TNT. Lots of them. Betty jumped back. "I found it!" she called. "Bombs! They've been making bombs!"

"And these plans!" Mr. Logan called. "Here's a plan of that bridge that blew up yesterday! They're the ones who did it, all right!"

"So let's get out of here!" Betty said, coming into the kitchen.

"Wait a minute. I just want to look around a little more. You take these plans and close the boxes. Now, don't worry. Mrs. Katz will give us lots of time to get out."

Downstairs, Mrs. Katz was watching out her window. Then she saw a cat out on the street. It was one of her cats! "Now, how did she get out?" Mrs. Katz asked herself. She turned around and looked at her front door. "That Mr. Logan!" she said. "He went off and left the door open, and now my kitty is out there all by herself. The next thing I know, she'll get hit by a car." Mrs. Katz put down her spoon and headed for the door.

She hurried out into the front hall, past the mailboxes, and down the front steps. "Here, kitty, kitty,"

she called. "Come back here, you silly little thing."

A red car came down the street. It pulled up in front of the building. Three men got out.

Mrs. Katz looked back. Oh, no! It was them! She grabbed her cat and ran back toward the building. Her feet pounded on the sidewalk. She gasped for breath. She hadn't run in so many years!

The men were taking their suitcases out of the car as she went by them. They looked at her in surprise as she ran gasping up the steps. Then they picked up their suitcases and went up the steps after her.

Mrs. Katz ran into her apartment. She grabbed her spoon and began to bang wildly on the water pipe.

Upstairs, Mr. Logan heard the pounding. "That's Mrs. Katz!" he called, running for the door. "Quick! Let's go! They're coming!"

Then he heard the men's footsteps on the stairs.

"Mrs. Rounds! Out the window!" he called. Then he dove out into the hall and closed the door.

The men came up the stairs, turned, and came down the hall. Mr. Logan was standing in front of his own door. "Good morning," he said. "Nice day, isn't it?"

"Yes, very nice," one of the men said. The other two kept on walking toward their door.

"Wait a minute!" Mr. Logan called after them. "I wanted to ask you something!"

The men came back and stood looking at him. "Well?" one of them asked.

"Oh .... How do you like your new apartment? Is everything OK?"

"Yes." The men turned to go.

"Wait!" Mr. Logan said again. "Some of the people in the building have been telling me that they've been having problems with ... with their water pipes. I'm filling in for the super this week. He's away this week. So I'm taking his place. Anyway, some of the people said that their water pipes have been banging. Have you had any problems with that?"

"That's the lady downstairs," one of the men said. "We saw her as we came in. She was banging on the water pipes with a spoon. She must be crazy or something."

"Oh, really?" Mr. Logan asked. "That must be Mrs. Katz. Thank you for telling me about that." The other two men were walking down the hall. "Well, if you have any problems, just call me," he yelled after them. "Anything at all. Just call me. I'm filling in for the super, and ...."

But the men were already unlocking their door.

Directions. Answer these questions about the chapter you have just read. Put an *x* in the box beside the best answer to each question.

1. (C) When did Betty get out of bed?
   - ☐ a. When Frank woke her up
   - ☐ b. When Lynn woke her up
   - ☐ c. When she knew that Frank was gone
   - ☐ d. When she heard the new men talking

2. (A) When Betty was pounding on the door of the men's apartment, Frank stood <u>with his mouth hanging open</u>, watching her. What does this mean?
   - ☐ a. He was so surprised at what she was doing that his mouth popped open.
   - ☐ b. He was so tired from getting up early that his mouth fell open.
   - ☐ c. He opened his mouth to shout for help.
   - ☐ d. He had to open his mouth wide for the dentist.

3. (D) Why did Mr. Logan change his mind about Frank?
   - ☐ a. He wanted to know what Frank could find out about the men.
   - ☐ b. He knew that Frank would never spy on anyone again.
   - ☐ c. He didn't care about his mailbox any more.
   - ☐ d. He decided that he liked having children around.

4. (A) Mr. Logan told Betty, "Two people could check out the apartment so much faster. I don't move around as well as I used to." What does this mean?

☐ a. He had too much to do.
☐ b. He felt that he was getting old and slow.
☐ c. He didn't want to move to a new apartment building.
☐ d. He didn't know his way around the building any more.

5. (C) When did Betty find out about the bomb at the airport?

☐ a. When she turned on the radio
☐ b. When the policeman told her on the phone
☐ c. When Mr. Logan and Mrs. Katz told her
☐ d. When she went out for the newspaper

6. (E) Why did Betty say she would help Mr. Logan check out the men's apartment?

☐ a. She wanted to make Mr. Logan happy.
☐ b. Frank asked her to do it.
☐ c. She wanted to keep Frank from doing it.
☐ d. She liked to do dangerous things.

7. (E) What did Betty and Mr. Logan find in the men's apartment?

☐ a. Guns
☐ b. Beds
☐ c. Heavy suitcases
☐ d. Plans and bombs

8. (B) Why did Mrs. Katz go out of the building instead of watching for the men?

    ☐ a. She saw the TV repair truck coming.
    ☐ b. She saw that one of her cats had got out.
    ☐ c. She got tired of waiting.
    ☐ d. She wanted to look at the red car.

9. (B) Why was Betty still in the men's apartment when they got back?

    ☐ a. She found out that they were good men after all.
    ☐ b. She wasn't scared of the men any more.
    ☐ c. Mrs. Katz didn't tell her in time that the men were coming.
    ☐ d. Mr. Logan took too much time getting out of the apartment.

10. (D) Why did Mr. Logan talk to the men in the hall?

    ☐ a. He liked to talk to people.
    ☐ b. He wanted to do a good job as a super.
    ☐ c. He wanted to give Betty time to get out the window.
    ☐ d. He wanted to ask them what they were up to.

Skills Used to Answer Questions

A. Recognizing Words in Context   B. Recalling Facts
C. Keeping Events in Order   D. Making Inferences
E. Understanding Main Ideas

Using Singular Subjects and Action Words

You know that subjects and action words can be singular or plural. Singular subjects name one person, place or thing. Plural subjects name more than one person, place or thing.

The subject and the action word in a sentence must *agree*. This means that if the subject is singular, the action word must be singular. If the subject is plural, the action word must be plural.

The examples below show how singular subjects and singular action words go together. The subject of each sentence is underlined once. The subject is singular. The action word in each sentence is underlined twice. The action word is singular, too.

The <u>boy</u> <u>stays</u> at home.

The <u>rock</u> <u>sinks</u> in the water.

The <u>girl</u> <u>listens</u> to the radio.

Always make sure that the subject and the action word in a sentence agree. If the subject is singular, the action word must be singular, too. One easy way to see if the singular subject and the action word agree is to check the last letter of the subject and of the action word. If the subject does *not* end in *s*, the action word probably should end in *s*.

Exercise 1

The subject of each sentence below is singular. Circle the singular action word. Then print the whole sentence. The first two have been done for you.

1. Mary (talks) / talk . *Mary talks.*

2. The baby (plays) / play . *The baby plays.*

3. The man [cleans / clean] . _____

4. Jack [turns / turn] . _____

5. The flower [bend / bends] . _____

6. The knife [cuts / cut] . _____

7. The cat [sleep / sleeps] . _____

8. The sun [shine / shines] . _____

9. The chair [break / breaks] . _____

10. The door $\begin{bmatrix} \text{opens} \\ \text{open} \end{bmatrix}$. _____

11. The bell $\begin{bmatrix} \text{rings} \\ \text{ring} \end{bmatrix}$. _____

12. The woman $\begin{bmatrix} \text{stands} \\ \text{stand} \end{bmatrix}$. _____

Exercise 2

Look at the pairs of sentences below. The first sentence of each pair has a plural subject and plural action word. The plural action word is underlined.

The second sentence of each pair has a singular subject. It needs a singular action word. The underlined action word in each first sentence is a clue to the missing action word in the second sentence.

Print the singular action word on the line after each singular subject. The first two have been done for you.

1. Cows <u>eat</u> grass.   (plural)

   A cow __*eats*_____ grass.   (singular)

2. The girls <u>lift</u> the barrel   (plural)

   Sandy __*lifts*_____the barrel.   (singular)

3. The boys <u>build</u> a sand castle.

   The boy _____ a sand castle.

4. The cars slide on the ice.

   The car _____ on the ice.

5. His brothers cover the pool every night.

   Bill _____ the pool every night.

6. Her grandparents smile at her.

   Her grandmother _____ at her.

7. Many people put sugar in their coffee.

   Ken _____ sugar in his coffee.

8. Her parents buy her everything.

   Her father _____ her everything.

9. The pipes bring the water into the houses.

   The pipe _____ the water into the house.

10. These shoes feel tight.

    This shoe _____ tight.

11. The chairs rock back and forth.

    The chair _____ back and forth.

12. The students sharpen their pencils.

    The student _____ her pencil.

Job Applications: Part One

When you go to apply for a job, you will usually have to do two things. You will meet the person who can hire you. And you probably will have to fill out a job *application.* The application is a form for giving information about yourself.

You should keep your application form as neat as possible. Always print the information the application asks for. And be sure to print only in the right space for each fact you are printing. You will usually have to print very small to fit your information in the right space.

The first part of a job application is given on the next page. This part of the application form asks you for personal information. Notice that the person who filled out this sample form printed all the information and kept it in the right spaces. Then read the information and look at the explanations that begin on this page.

Position Desired. Position means a job. In the space for position desired, you would print the name of the job you are applying for.

1. What job is the person who filled out the form applying for?

_____

APPLICATION FOR EMPLOYMENT

POSITION DESIRED _mechanic_

PERSONAL INFORMATION

DATE
Month _June_ Day _21_ Year _1993_

SOCIAL SECURITY NUMBER
_803-80-7653_

NAME
Last _Edwards_ First _Thomas_ Middle Initial _R._

ADDRESS
_23_ Street _Pine St._ City _Syracuse_ State _N.Y._ Zip _03214_

NUMBER OF DEPENDENTS _3_

MARITAL STATUS (check one)
Single ☐
Married ☑
Divorced ☐

PHONE _546-2102_

U.S. CITIZEN (check one)
Yes ☑
No ☐

DATE OF BIRTH
Month _March_ Day _6_ Year _1945_

Date. In this space you would give the date of the day that you fill out the application. Notice that the form asks you to give the month, day and year. The words at the top of the space tell you where to put each part of the date.

Social Security Number. Copy your number very carefully from your Social Security card. Always bring your card when you go to apply for a job.

Name. In the next space, you would print your name. Check the form to see in what order it asks you to print your name. This form is like most job applications. It asks you to print your *last* name first.

2. What is the last name of the person who filled out this form?

_____

Address. In this space you would give your full address. After the number and street where you live, you would print the city, state and zip code.

3. What is the name of the city in which the person who filled out this form lives?

_____

Phone Number. In this space, give the phone number at which you can be reached most easily. If you get the job you are applying for, the person who hires you will tell you by phone. Be sure that each number is clear.

Number of Dependents. Dependents are people you support. In the space for the number of your dependents you would write the total number of people you support. This would be all the people who depend on your pay to live. Examples are children, a husband, a wife, a parent or anyone else you support.

4. How many dependents does Thomas Edwards have? Write the number.

_____

Marital Status. This means whether or not you are married *now.* You must check only one box. If you have never been married, or if you were married and your husband or wife died, you should check the *Single* box. Otherwise, check the box that tells if you are married now or divorced now.

5. Is Thomas Edwards married now? Circle your answer.

Yes   No

U.S. Citizen. Check only one box to tell whether you are a citizen of the United States or not.

Date of Birth. In this space you would fill in the day, month, day and year that you were born. Notice the words at the top of the box that tell you where to put each part of the date.

Filling Out a Job Application

Use the facts below to fill out the first part of the sample job application that is given on the next page.

Position Desired

switchboard operator

Personal Information

Date: July 1, 1993

Social Security Number: 272-50-8253

Name: Sarah A. Biggs

Address: 944 Wood Avenue
Akron, Ohio 45126

Phone: 782-5946

Number of Dependents: 1

Marital Status: Single

U.S. Citizen: Yes

Date of Birth: February 20, 1957

APPLICATION FOR EMPLOYMENT

POSITION DESIRED _____

PERSONAL INFORMATION

SOCIAL SECURITY NUMBER

DATE Month   Day   Year

NAME Last   First   Middle Initial

ADDRESS Street   City   State   Zip

NUMBER OF DEPENDENTS

PHONE

MARITAL STATUS (check one)
Single ☐
Married ☐
Divorced ☐

DATE OF BIRTH   Month   Day   Year

U.S. CITIZEN (check one)
Yes ☐
No ☐

5

Hostage!

Study the words in the box. Then read the sentences below with your teacher. Look carefully at the words with lines under them.

animals	garbage	ledge	neckties
basement	handcuffs	lose	ransom
broadcast	heavily	loudspeaker	rattled
clawing	hostage	million	stumbled
froze	knock	murderers	warning

1. Below her were the stairs down to the <u>basement</u>.
2. The <u>garbage</u> cans were put there.
3. She climbed out onto the narrow <u>ledge</u>.
4. She stood up. And <u>froze</u>.
5. The fire escape shook and <u>rattled</u>.
6. It must have been a <u>warning</u>!
7. She <u>stumbled</u> over to Betty and Mr. Logan.
8. "You're all <u>murderers</u>!" Betty shouted.
9. We will be holding the city for <u>ransom</u>.
10. TV stations will <u>broadcast</u> our ransom note.
11. We want five <u>million</u> dollars.
12. The city will <u>lose</u> millions of dollars.
13. <u>Knock</u>! Knock! A little fist pounded on the door.
14. Something was on him—all over him— <u>Animals</u>!
15. They were <u>clawing</u>, screaming, jumping—
16. "Stand back!" the man yelled. "I've got a <u>hostage</u>!"
17. A <u>loudspeaker</u> boomed through the window.
18. He leaned <u>heavily</u> on her.
19. They grabbed the man and put <u>handcuffs</u> on him.
20. We got them all tied up with your <u>neckties</u>.

Betty heard Mr. Logan shout. The men were coming! She was trapped!

The window! It was her only chance! She ran to the window and threw it open.

It was a long way to the ground.

She was only on the second floor, but below her were the stairs down to the basement. The garbage cans were put there. And around them was a fence. At the top of each fence post was a sharp spike. Betty felt as if every spike was pointing right at her.

She couldn't reach the fire escape from the window. She stopped. She had to think! There must be some other way to get out.

But then she heard the men's voices. They were talking to Mr. Logan—right out in the hall! They were coming closer!

Quickly, Betty climbed out the window. She climbed out onto the narrow ledge on the outside of the apartment building. She stood up.

And froze.

She couldn't move. She could hardly breathe.

The fire escape was only a few feet away. If she took just a few steps along the ledge, she could reach it. Then she could get up on it and get to Mr. Logan's window.

But she couldn't move. She was frozen. The ground was pulling at her .... And those spikes ....

Then she heard the men's voices again. They were in the apartment!

"Hey!" one man said. "Who left the window open?

Can't you even remember to shut the window when we go out?"

"Oh, shut up, Larry," another man said. "You're always going on about something. If you don't want the window open, then shut it!"

Betty heard the man coming across the room. She held herself flat against the side of the building. She held her breath. If the man leaned out the open window .... He would see her standing there—only a few inches away.

The man's hands came up to the top of the window. They waited for a moment. Betty was dizzy with fear. Then the window slammed shut.

Betty let her breath out slowly. She was safe for the moment. But she had to get out of there!

She *had* to make herself move.

She stood flat against the building, trying not to look down, trying not to think. She let her mind go. Suddenly she could hear a voice in her head. It was the voice of the woman on the subway, singing,

"Swing low, sweet chariot,

Coming for to carry me home ...."

She thought about how calm that woman had been in the dark subway. Betty began to feel better. If that woman could do it, *she* could!

Slowly, she pushed one foot to the right, along the ledge. So far, so good. She slid herself along—one inch, two inches. She moved her foot again, a little more this time. She slid herself over, then dragged her left foot over. She was moving! She could do it! She moved her right foot over and began to slide herself over when—her foot slipped!

The ground below her seemed to turn. Her head

spun. She tried to push herself back against the building. But the ground pulled at her.... She was falling.... The spikes on the fence were pointing up at her....

The fire escape! It was her only chance! She threw herself at it, pushing herself out into the air. Her hands reached out for it, reaching, reaching—and got it! She grabbed the railing and held tightly onto it. Her legs swung down under her. Clang! Bang! The fire escape shook and rattled. Betty hung on for dear life. But the noise! The men would hear her!

She saw Mr. Logan's face in his window. He threw the window open. Then he climbed out onto the fire escape and ran toward her.

Mr. Logan grabbed the railing with one hand. Then he leaned over the railing and held out his other hand to Betty.

Betty let go of the railing with one hand and grabbed Mr. Logan's hand. He pulled her up until she could get her leg over the railing. Clang! Clang! She got her other leg over the railing. Bang! It made so much noise!

And then she heard another noise. It was the sound of another window opening.

"What's going on out there?" someone shouted. Betty looked back. One of the men was leaning out the window in back of her and Mr. Logan. "What do you think you're doing?"

"Who's out there?" Another man came to the window. "What are they doing out there?"

Mr. Logan and Betty climbed in quickly through Mr. Logan's window. If only the men wouldn't....

"Hey! Our window was open! She must have been

the one who was in here! Get her!"

Betty and Mr. Logan looked at each other wildly. What should they do? Should they go back out the window? But someone was already pounding on the door. And one man was still leaning out of the other window—with a gun ready in his hand.

"Open this door!" a man was shouting. "Open this door, or we'll break it down!"

Mr. Logan went to the door and opened it. "What's the matter?" he asked. "What—" Two men pushed him back into the apartment. The door slammed shut behind them.

"All right, what's this all about?" one of the men asked. "What were you two doing on the fire escape?"

"Why, we were just—"

"Don't mess with me, old man! Someone has been in our apartment! Someone has been messing around with our stuff! It was you, wasn't it? And then all this talk in the hall. . . . You were just giving her time to get out!"

"Hey! I just thought of something!" the other man said. "That old lady! The one who was banging on the pipes! It must have been a warning! She must have been warning them that we were coming!"

"Get her up here!" the first man said. "Get Larry, too. We'll have to think about what to do with them." He stood with his gun pointed at Mr. Logan. "Don't move. You stand still, too, lady."

The other man went out. He came back a moment later, pushing Mrs. Katz in front of him. The third man came in with them.

Mrs. Katz was shaking all over and crying. "Oh, Mrs. Rounds . . . . Oh, Mr. Logan . . . . I'm so sorry! My kitty got out and I just had to go get her. And the men came while I was outside. Oh, I'm so sorry—"

"Shut up!" one of the men yelled. "Get over there with them!" He gave Mrs. Katz a push. She stumbled over to Betty and Mr. Logan. Betty put her arms around her and hugged her.

"Well, what are we going to do with them?" one man asked. "Kill them now, or—"

"Oh!" Mrs. Katz gasped. She hid her face against Betty.

"We don't have to do anything with them yet. We can just hold them till after tomorrow. After tomorrow—"

"You won't get away with this!" Mr. Logan cut in. "We know what you're up to! We saw your plans! We know that you stopped the subway! And blew up the bridge! And put a bomb at the airport!"

"You're all murderers!" Betty shouted. "All those people in the subway! All those people killed and hurt! You murdered them! Murderers!"

"Hey, lady, calm down!" one of the men said. "How were *we* to know that all those people were going to go crazy like that? If they had stayed quiet, no one would have been hurt!"

"Hey, cut it!" one of the other men said. But the third man went on.

"See, we were more careful with the bridge job. We moved up the time so that it wouldn't blow at rush hour. And the airport . . . . We did that job really early in the morning so there wouldn't be so many people around. We—"

"Larry! Shut up!" the first man snapped. "Are you crazy?"

"But why? Why?" Betty asked. "*Why* are you doing all this?"

"Just wait till tomorrow!" said the man named Larry. "Tomorrow we're going to—"

"Larry! Can it!" the second man said, grabbing his arm. "You talk too much! Now, shut up!"

"Oh, let him talk," the first man said. "Why not tell them about it? What can happen? What can they do to stop us now?"

The second man stepped back. "OK. But I don't like it. I don't like it one bit." He went over and stood by the window.

For a moment, it was quiet in the room. Then Mr. Logan asked, "Well? What will happen tomorrow?"

"The city will be ours!" Larry said. "We will be holding the city for ransom."

"The city? Holding the city for ransom?" Mr. Logan asked. "What do you mean?"

"Tomorrow, every radio and TV station will broadcast our ransom note. We want five million dollars! If we don't get it... the city will stop!"

"Oh, dear, oh, dear." Mrs. Katz started to cry again. Betty hugged her. She wanted to cry, too, but she wouldn't let herself do it.

"Five million dollars? Where will the city get that kind of money?" Mr. Logan asked.

"That's their problem," the first man said, walking over to stand next to Larry. "But they'll get it. If they don't, the city will stop till they do."

"That's right," Larry said. "We gave them a taste of what we can do. A subway line.... A bridge.... The airport.... People are already starting to be afraid to go anywhere."

Betty thought about the people she had seen on the way to work. The man was right. They were afraid.

"That was only a taste," Larry went on. "If we don't get our money, we'll stop the city cold. No subways, no trains, no planes. People won't dare to use their cars. No one will dare to go *anywhere!*"

"You won't get away with this!" Mr. Logan shouted. "It won't work!"

"Oh, yes, it will," Larry smiled. "No one will go to work. No trucks will come in with food or other things. The stores won't have anything to sell .... or anyone to sell things to. The city will lose millions of dollars every day that they wait. It won't take long. They'll give in."

"We'll get our money," the other man said. "It's only a matter of time. And *we* can wait. *They* can't."

The men stopped talking. Betty and Mr. Logan could think of nothing to say. The only sound was Mrs. Katz's crying. It was very quiet in the room.

Suddenly, Betty heard something. It was a very soft sound. A sound she knew well.

It was Lynn's footsteps ... coming down the hall.

"No! No!" Betty thought to herself. "No, Lynn! Go away!" She tried to *will* Lynn not to come to the door. She closed her eyes and held Mrs. Katz's hands tightly. "Please, Lynn!" she thought. "Please don't come here."

The little footsteps came closer.

The men heard them now. They stood quietly, waiting.

The footsteps came right up to the door and stopped.

No one moved. A long minute went by. Betty was shaking all over. "Oh, please, Lynn . . . ."

Knock! Knock! A little fist was pounding on the door.

The men looked at each other.

Knock! Knock! Knock! The little fist pounded again.

"Go get it," the man by the window said quietly. Larry went to the door. He opened it wide.

Splat! Something flew through the air and hit him in the face.

"Hey!"

"Ow!"

"What the—"

Everything happened at once.

Larry fell over backwards. Something was on him—all over him—everywhere— Animals! A river of animals ran into the room! A million of them! Everywhere! Clawing, screaming, jumping—

"Cats!" yelled the man by the window. But before he could take a step, a cat flew through the open window right at him. It landed on his head, claws ready. The man stumbled and went down, screaming.

"My cats!" yelled Mrs. Katz. The door slammed shut. The trapped cats ran everywhere.

"Quick, Mom! Hit them!" yelled a voice from the window. "Get the men while they're down!" Frank was climbing in from the fire escape.

Betty turned to look at him. The man who had been by the window was getting up! He was reaching for his gun! Betty grabbed a chair and swung it. She hit the man across the back as hard as she could. He went down again. Betty slammed the chair down hard

again. The man lay still.

Mr. Logan grabbed another chair. He swung it at the last man before the man could turn around. The man fell across the table and went down with a crash.

Larry was trying to get to his feet. Mr. Logan grabbed the gun that Larry had dropped. Slam! As Larry stood up, Mr. Logan hit him on the back of the head. Larry fell in a heap. He did not move.

Betty ran to Frank. "Are you all right? Where's Lynn? Lynn, where are you? Oh, children!"

"My cats! Oh, Blackie! Fuzz-ball! What are you

doing here?" Mrs. Katz called.

Mr. Logan checked Larry to see if he was out cold. Then he went on to the man by the window.

Betty took a quick look at the last man. He lay under the table, his arms and legs thrown every which way.

"Is he dead, Mom?" Frank asked. His voice was shaking.

"No, I don't think so," Betty said. She bent down and hugged Frank. Then she looked around the room. "Lynn, where are you?" she called. She heard someone move near her. "Lynn?" She turned to look.

She was looking into the mouth of a gun.

"Don't move, lady," the man said. He got up, pulling himself up by the table. Then he pointed with his gun for Betty to stand up. "All right, everyone," the man said. "If anyone moves, this lady gets it. You!" He pointed at Mr. Logan. "Drop that gun!" The gun hit the floor.

The man held his gun against Betty's back. "Everyone over there by the wall!" he snapped. "You, too, kid! If anyone moves, it's all over for Mom, here. We're just going to wait quietly till my friends wake up." He looked down at the cats. They were all in the middle of the room now, eating a big fish that was lying on the floor. "After that little trick," he said, "I don't think we'll wait till tomorrow to get rid of you. All of you!"

Mr. Logan, Mrs. Katz, and Frank lined up by the wall. Betty stood facing them. She could feel the gun sticking into her back.

She looked at the two men lying on the floor. When would they wake up? What would happen when they did?

They stood still in the quiet room. All they could hear was their own breathing, and cars going by on the street.

Suddenly, one car stopped in front of the building. A door slammed. Who was it? Would someone come into the building? Could they call for help?

They could hear footsteps coming up the front steps below the window. "Don't anyone move! Don't anyone make a sound, or the lady gets it!" the man said from behind Betty. The gun stuck harder into her back.

A man came up the stairs. He went by, up to the next floor. A moment later, he came back down. He stopped. Then the footsteps came down the hall, up to the door.

Knock! Knock!

No one moved.

Knock! Knock! "Anyone there?" a man's voice called. "This is the police!"

Betty gasped. The gun was sticking into her back so hard that it hurt. "Stand back!" the man behind her yelled. "I've got a hostage! The lady gets it if you try to stop me! Clear the hall! Get your people out of the building! I'm coming out, and I'm taking the hostage with me! Clear the building, and make it fast!"

The footsteps ran back down the hall. A moment later, the car door slammed again. The car pulled out and moved a little way down the street.

Betty looked at Frank. She could hear her heart pounding. Minute after minute went by. What was going to happen?

Suddenly a loudspeaker boomed through the open window. "The building is clear! No one is going to shoot!" the voice said. "Give yourself up! Come out quietly, and no one will shoot!"

"Stand back!" the man shouted toward the window. Suddenly he put his arm around Betty's neck. He leaned heavily on her. "Walk over to the window! Slowly!" he snapped.

Betty walked toward the window. The man stumbled along behind her, leaning on her. He could hardly walk. He must have hurt his leg, Betty thought. But the gun never moved from her back.

"I'm coming out!" the man shouted out the window. "No one stop me, or this lady gets it!" He turned his head a little. "Old man! Do you know how to drive?"

"Me?" asked Mr. Logan. "Yes, I can drive."

"Get the keys off him," the man said, pointing with his gun at the man by him on the floor. Then the gun was in Betty's back again.

Mr. Logan bent down and reached into the man's pockets. At last he found the keys. He stood up. "OK."

"All right! I'm coming out!" the man shouted. "I'm bringing two hostages with me! We're going to get into that red car! No one try to stop us!" He pushed on Betty's neck, and she turned around. "Let's go!"

Slowly, they moved across the room. The cats walked around them and rubbed against their legs. The man stumbled, pulling hard on Betty's neck. "Get those cats out of my way!" he snapped.

Frank and Mrs. Katz ran over and tried to get the cats to move. They grabbed and pulled at them. But there were so many of them!

At last Betty and the man had reached the door. "Open the door. Then close it behind us," the man told

Frank. He pushed Betty through the door. Some of the cats ran past them and ran down the stairs.

Slowly, Betty and the man made their way down the hall. Then down the stairs, one by one. Mr. Logan walked close to their side. Slowly, slowly, they walked toward the front door.

Betty was so tired from holding the man up. What if she stumbled and fell? Would he shoot her?

They walked out of the building. Betty looked around, surprised. Police were everywhere! All around them, police cars were parked and the police stood ready. But they were all standing back, waiting.

The red car was right in front of them. Waiting to take them—where?

Now they were going down the front steps. One

step. Another step. Then—

"Ow!" the man screamed. He fell backwards, grabbing for something that was clawing at his face. Betty was thrown down the steps. Bang! The gun went off into the air.

Mr. Logan turned fast and jumped on the man, grabbing his arms. The police rushed over. They grabbed the man and put handcuffs on him. One policewoman helped Betty up. "Are you all right, lady?" she asked.

"Yes, yes. Mr. Logan? Are *you* all right?" Betty asked. "Oh, I was scared you'd been shot. What happened?"

"This cat!" Mr. Logan said. "It came right out of the sky and landed on his head!"

They looked up. Frank was standing above them on the fire escape. He was grinning from ear to ear.

"Frank! Did you drop that cat down here?" Betty called.

"Of course! I knew it wouldn't get hurt. Cats always land on their feet."

"But your mother!" Mr. Logan said. "She could have been shot!"

"Well, I knew that the man would fall down, with that hurt leg and all. It worked one time, so I thought it would work again," Frank said. But he wasn't grinning any more.

"Frank, where is Lynn? Have you seen her?" Betty asked.

"Oh, she's back in our apartment. I told her to go back up there and lock the door as soon as she threw the fish. I'll go get her." Frank started to run up the fire escape.

"Wait, Frank!" Mr. Logan called. "What about those other men? They might wake up any time now!"

"Oh, don't worry, Mr. Logan. Mrs. Katz and I got them all tied up with your neckties." Frank climbed up the fire escape to the third floor.

The police were already crowding into the building. Betty and Mr. Logan led them up the stairs to Mr. Logan's apartment. Frank and Lynn were waiting for them in the hall.

They opened the door. There was Mrs. Katz, sitting in a chair, with two cats in her lap. More cats were rubbing around her legs. Two guns were lying on the table in front of her. And the two men were all tied up at her feet.

Betty showed the police the men's apartment. She showed them the plans, and the box of bombs. Mr. Logan came in, and they told the police about what the men had told them.

"But how did you know?" a policewoman asked. "What made you come in here and look?"

"Well, it was Frank," Betty said. "He was the one who thought it out. We didn't believe him. But Mr. Logan said we'd better check it out. *I* came along just to keep Frank from doing it." Betty told them about how the men had come back, and how she had gone out the window. "So they had us all in Mr. Logan's apartment. And then all these cats came in."

"That worked really well, didn't it?" Frank said. "I saw Mom on the fire escape, and I heard the men yelling. I had to think what to do. Mrs. Katz's door was open. The cats were all over the place downstairs. So I got the fish out of our refrigerator. I told Lynn to get all those cats upstairs with the fish. And I told her to throw the fish into Mr. Logan's apartment. Then I put one cat in a bag and ran upstairs and came down on the fire escape."

"Without making any noise?" Betty asked.

"Oh, I do it all the time. You know—when I'm ... oh ... seeing what people are doing. Then when Lynn threw the fish, I threw the other cat in through the window. I thought it would be good to have cats coming from everywhere at once."

"Yes, that was something, all right," Mr. Logan said. "It gave us a chance to knock out two of the men," he told the police. "But the last one came to and got his gun back. So we were back where we started. And then a policeman came."

"That was me," one policeman said. "I talked to this lady on the phone this morning. I felt bad about cutting you off. So when some of the cars got back from the airport, I came down to talk to you. Your little girl told me where to find you. Then I heard that man yell, 'Hostage!' I knew we had some work to do."

"So then you came out of the building," another policeman said. "We didn't know what we were going to do. But we were waiting for a break. And then that cat fell out of the sky."

"That's quite a boy you've got there, lady," a policewoman said. "I don't think I would dare use his way to save hostages. But I'm glad it worked out."

The police cars took the men away. Two of the police stayed to check out the men's apartment. Betty, Mr. Logan, and the children helped Mrs. Katz round up her cats and get them back into her apartment.

When the last cat was in, Betty said, "Mrs. Katz? Mr. Logan? Why don't the two of you have dinner with us tonight? I'll have to get the place cleaned up a bit. And we won't have fish! But it would be nice to have you eat with us."

"That would be fun," Mr. Logan said.

"That sounds very nice," Mrs. Katz said. "What time would you like us to come?"

"Around 6:00? Would that be all right?"

"Sounds good," said Mr. Logan. "I think we'll have a lot to talk about!"

Betty hurried about happily, cleaning her apartment. "We'll have to go shopping," she told the children. "There's a lot of things I need. We'll have a big dinner. We haven't had a dinner party in a long time."

"That's super, Mom!" Frank said. Lynn jumped around happily.

Betty stopped and looked at them. "I want to know one more thing," she said. "Lynn, when the policeman came to the door, why didn't you tell him about the men with guns?"

"Oh, Mom," Frank cut in. "She didn't *know*! I didn't tell her! I just told her to throw that fish into Mr. Logan's apartment, then run upstairs. I told her it was a trick on Mr. Logan. I didn't want her to be scared, did I?"

Betty smiled. "You think of everything, Frank. But why didn't *you* call the police?"

Frank looked surprised. "I never thought of that!" he said.

"Ask her!" Lynn said suddenly.

"Ask me what?" Betty asked.

The children looked at each other. Then Frank said, "We want to know one thing, too. Are we really going to move out of the city?"

Betty bent down and hugged them both. "You really don't want to, do you? This *is* home, isn't it? Well, we won't move. We kept those men from stopping the city. And if the city can keep going . . . . Well, we'll just have to keep going with it."

As she went on with her work, she found herself singing. But now it was a happy song.

"Swing low, sweet chariot,
Coming for to carry me home . . . ."

Directions. Answer these questions about the chapter you have just read. Put an *x* in the box beside the best answer to each question.

1. (A) Betty climbed out on the narrow ledge on the outside of the building. She stood up. Then she <u>froze</u>. What does this mean?

   ☐ a. She got caught in an ice storm.
   ☐ b. She was so scared that she couldn't move.
   ☐ c. She stood still so that she wouldn't fall.
   ☐ d. She didn't have any warm clothes.

2. (C) When did the men come into Mr. Logan's apartment?

   ☐ a. When they heard Mrs. Katz banging on the pipe.
   ☐ b. When they saw that Betty was out on the ledge.
   ☐ c. When they saw that their window had been left open.
   ☐ d. When they saw Betty and Mr. Logan on the fire escape.

3. (A) Larry said, "We gave them a taste of what we can do." What does this mean?

☐ a. They showed the city just a little bit of what they can do.
☐ b. They have done everything they can do.
☐ c. They have made something good for the people to eat.
☐ d. They have found out what kind of things the city likes them to do.

4. (E) Why did the men want to stop the city?

☐ a. They were mad at someone.
☐ b. They liked to hurt people.
☐ c. They wanted to make the city pay them a lot of money.
☐ d. They wanted to take over the radio and TV stations.

5. (C) When Larry opened the door

☐ a. Lynn led the cats to Mr. Logan's door.
☐ b. Lynn threw the fish at Larry.
☐ c. Frank came down the fire escape.
☐ d. Frank threw one cat in the window.

6. (B) Why did the policeman happen to come to the apartment building?

☐ a. He knew that the men were planning to stop the city.
☐ b. He knew that someone was holding Betty hostage.
☐ c. Frank called the police station.
☐ d. Betty had called him that morning.

7. (B) How did Frank stop the man who was holding Betty hostage?

☐ a. He took the man's gun.
☐ b. He hit the man with a chair.
☐ c. He dropped a cat on the man's head.
☐ d. He tied the man up with Mr. Logan's neckties.

8. (D) Why did Betty ask Mr. Logan and Mrs. Katz to come to dinner?

☐ a. She thought they should celebrate.
☐ b. She wanted them to help her eat the fish.
☐ c. She was scared to be all by herself in the apartment.
☐ d. She liked to give a lot of big dinner parties.

9. (D) How did Betty change, after all she had been through?

- ☐ a. She was scared to go anywhere.
- ☐ b. She became braver.
- ☐ c. She became sadder.
- ☐ d. She was mean to her children.

10. (E) What was the main thing that made Betty so happy at the end of the story?

- ☐ a. She liked to go shopping.
- ☐ b. She liked to clean her apartment.
- ☐ c. She knew that nothing bad would happen in the city again.
- ☐ d. She knew that she was strong enough to live in the city.

Skills Used to Answer Questions

A. Recognizing Words in Context   B. Recalling Facts
C. Keeping Events in Order   D. Making Inferences
E. Understanding Main Ideas

Using Plural Subjects and Action Words

You know that the subject and the action word in a sentence must agree. You have seen how a singular action word goes with a singular subject.

Each example below shows how a plural action word goes with a plural subject. The subject of each sentence is underlined once. The subject is plural so it ends in *s*. The action word is underlined twice. The action word is plural, so it does not end in *s*.

My friends leave their door unlocked.

The doctors think that he'll be fine.

The trains usually run on time.

Always make sure that the subject and the action word in a sentence agree. If the subject is plural, the action word must be plural, too. One easy way to see if the plural subject and the action word agree is to check the last letter of the subject and of the action word. If the subject ends in *s*, the action word probably should not end in *s*.

Exercise 1

The subjects of the following sentences are plural. Circle the plural action word. Then print the whole sentence. The first two have been done for you.

1. The children (look) / looks

   The children look.

2. The trains   stops   / (stop)

_____*The trains stop.*_____

3. The sisters   listen   /   listens

_____

4. The dogs   runs   /   run

_____

5. The ducks   swim   /   swims

_____

6. The boys   waves   /   wave

_____

7. The beds   sags   /   sag

_____

8. The leaves   falls   /   fall

_____

9. The plants   grow   /   grows

_____

10. The airplanes   rise   /   rises

_____

Exercise 2

Look at the pairs of sentences below. The first sentence of each pair has a singular subject and a singular action word. The singular action word is underlined.

The second sentence of each pair has a plural subject. It needs a plural action word. The underlined action word in each first sentence is a clue to the missing action word in the second sentence.

Print the plural action word on the line after each plural subject. The first two have been done for you.

1. An apple <u>makes</u> a good snack.   (singular)

   Apples_____*make*_____a good snack.   (plural)

2. The rose <u>smells</u> good.   (singular)

   The roses _____*smell*_____ good.   (plural)

3. A lime <u>tastes</u> good in that drink.

   Limes _____good in those drinks.

4. The woman <u>dials</u> the phone.

   The women _____ the phones.

5. The clerk <u>sweeps</u> the floor.

   The clerks _____the floor.

6. The cook <u>cuts</u> the bread.

   The cooks _____the bread.

7. The fireman <u>answers</u> the call.

   The firemen _____the call.

8. The plane <u>arrives</u> on time.

   The planes _____on time.

9. The clock <u>ticks</u> loudly.

   The clocks _____ loudly.

10. The phone <u>rings</u> constantly.

    The phones _____constantly.

Here are the steps to follow in making the subject and the action word of a sentence agree:
1. Find the subject of the sentence.
2. Decide whether the subject is singular or plural.
3. Make the action word singular if the subject is singular. Singular action words usually end in *s*.
4. Make the action word plural if the subject is plural. Plural action words usually do not end in *s*.

Exercise 3

Look at the pairs of sentences on the next page. The underlined action word in each first sentence is a clue to the missing action word in each second sentence.

Print a plural action word if the subject of the second sentence is plural. Print a singular action word if the subject of the second sentence is singular. The first two have been done for you.

1. The mother <u>holds</u> the baby.

    The mothers _____*hold*_____ the babies.

2. The policemen <u>hear</u> the noise.

    The policeman _____*hears*_____ the noise.

3. The cloud <u>hides</u> the sun.

    The clouds_____the sun.

4. His brothers <u>stay</u> behind.

    His brother _____ behind.

5. The teachers <u>close</u> the window.

    The teacher_____the window.

6. Her sister <u>gives</u> her gifts.

    Her sisters_____her gifts.

7. The branch <u>scrapes</u> against the window.

    The branches _____ against the window.

8. The students <u>write</u> often.

    The student_____often.

9. The cake <u>smells</u> good.

   The cakes _____ good.

10. The girls <u>jump</u> from the rock.

   The girl _____ from the rock.

Job Applications: Part Two

You have seen how to fill out the first part of a job application. The second part of the application form asks for information about your work experience.

This second part will be easier for you to fill out if you are prepared. There are some questions that all job applications ask you. This means you can write down the information you need to answer these questions ahead of time. You can bring the answers with you every time you go to apply for a job. If you copy your information from your paper, you can fill out a job application more quickly and easily.

The five things you need to know to fill out almost every job application are:

1. the name, address and phone number of each employer you worked for
2. the position you had there
3. the dates you had the position
4. how much you were paid
5. your reason for leaving each position

A sample of the second part of a job application is given on the pages that follow. You can see that the application has two headings: "Employment Record" and "References."

EMPLOYMENT RECORD (List last three employers, starting with last one first.)

(1)DATE Month Year	(2)NAME AND ADDRESS OF EMPLOYER	(3)PHONE	(4)POSITION	(5)PAY	(6)REASON FOR LEAVING
From June 1981 To present	Fred Collin's Pontiac 20 Grove St. Syracuse, N.Y.	273-9438	mechanic	$400 per week	higher pay
From July 1972 To June 1981	Anderson's Garage 43 Eilers Ave. Syracuse, N.Y.	835-2690	mechanic	$310 per week	better job
From March 1965 To July 1972	Ed's Garage 86 Orange St. Utica, N.Y.	786-3200	assistant mechanic	$270 per week	moved

REFERENCES

NAME	ADDRESS	PHONE	JOB TITLE AND EMPLOYER
Charles Hanson	36 Blossom Rd. Syracuse, N.Y.	546-3894	head mechanic Anderson's Garage

DATE June 21, 1993   SIGNATURE Thomas R. Edwards

This is one of the most important parts of a job application. It shows how much job experience you have. We have added numbers to the second part of the sample application form to show you how it was filled out.

Employer. On this part of a job application, employer means the company you worked for. Columns 2 and 3 ask you to give the name, address and phone number of your last three employers.

Most job applications tell you to begin with your *last* job. This means you should print the name of your last employer first. Then put your next-to-the-last job second, and so on. If you are working now, list the job you have now in the first space.

Date. In Column 1, the form asks you to give the months and years that you worked for each employer. Put the date you started in the space marked "From." Put the date you left in the space marked "To."

You can see that Thomas Edwards is working now. He printed "present" in the space for the last date of his last job. This means he is still working for that employer. He is working for Fred Collin's Pontiac *now*, or *at present.*

Position. In Column 4, print the name of the position or job you have, or have had, with each employer.

1. Print the word that tells you what position Thomas Edwards had at Anderson's Garage.

Pay. In Column 5, tell how much you got paid for each job. Tell whether you were paid by the hour, by the week, or by the month.

2. How was Thomas Edwards paid? Circle your answer.

By the hour   By the week   By the month

Reason for leaving. In Column 6, print one or two words that explain why you left each job. If you got a better job, print "better job." If you got more pay somewhere else, print "higher pay." Keep your explanation short.

3. Copy the one word that tells why Thomas Edwards left his job at Ed's Garage.

_____

References

A *reference* is someone who knows you and will recommend you for a job. A reference should be someone outside your family. The best reference for a job is someone you have worked for before. Choose someone who will say that you are a good worker and a responsible person. Put down the person's name, address, phone number, job title and employer.

This application asks for three references. If you don't have three, put down as many as you can. You should have at least one reference. If you cannot give the names of three people you have worked for, put down the name of a teacher or someone in your neighborhood who knows you.

4. How many references does Thomas Edwards have?

_____

Date and Signature

At the bottom of the application, put the date you filled out the application. Then write your name on the line for "Signature." A signature must always be written, not printed.

Filling Out a Job Application

Use the facts below to fill out the second part
Sarah Biggs's job application which is given
pages 169 and 170.

Employment Record

Last employer

Manson Company
Address: 86 Lake Drive
Akron, Ohio 45120

Phone: 487-6400

Dates: From March 1985 to the present

Position: switchboard operator

Pay: $350 per week

Reason for leaving: moved

Next-to-last employer

Chase and Sons
Address: 95 Vine Street
Akron, Ohio 45122

Phone: 396-5430

Dates: From March 1980 to March 1985

Position: switchboard operator

Pay: $300 per week

Reason for leaving: poor benefits

References

Ms. Jane Anders
95 Vine Street
Akron Ohio 45122

Phone: 396-5430

Job title and employer:

Supervisor, Chase and Sons

Ms. Martha McHughes
95 Vine Street
Akron Ohio 45122

Phone: 396-5430

Job title and employer:

Personnel Director, Chase and Sons

Mr. Peter Hutton
86 Lake Drive
Akron Ohio 45120

Phone: 487-6400

Job title and employer:

Personnel Manager, Manson Company

EMPLOYMENT RECORD (List last three employers, starting with last one first.)

DATE		NAME AND ADDRESS OF EMPLOYER	PHONE	POSITION	PAY	REASON FOR LEAVING
Month Year						
From						
To						
From						
To						
From						
To						

REFERENCES

NAME	ADDRESS		PHONE	JOB TITLE AND EMPLOYER

DATE _____ SIGNATURE _____

To the Instructor

To the Instructor

Purpose of the Series

Teachers charged with the responsibility of providing instruction for adults and older students with reading difficulties face a major problem: the lack of suitable materials. Stories written at the appropriate level of maturity are too difficult; stories easy enough to read independently are too childish.

The stories in the Adult Learner Series were written to solve the readability problem. The plots and characters in these stories are suitable for adults and older students, yet the stories can be read easily by very low-level readers.

The principal goal of the series is to provide interest and enjoyment for these readers. To this end, every attempt has been made to create a pleasant reading experience and to avoid frustration. The plots move quickly but are kept simple; a few characters are introduced and developed slowly; the same characters are utilized throughout a text; sentence structure and vocabulary are carefully monitored.

A secondary goal is to help adults explore and develop everyday life skills. Lessons and exercises about a variety of life skills provide adults and older students with the basic competencies they need for success in this fast-paced world.

Rounding out the structure of the series are exercises for developing vocabulary skills, comprehension skills, and language skills.

Reading Level

The stories in the Adult Learner Series are all written at second grade reading level. It should be kept in mind, however, that the stories were written for adults: people with a wider range of experience and larger speaking and listening vocabularies than those of elementary school children. Thus, there are some words and some events which might present difficulties for elementary school students but which should not pose problems for older beginning readers.

Besides the slightly increased complexity of vocabulary and plot, the writing style itself has been adapted for older beginning readers. Every effort was made to make the prose sound natural while maintaining simplicity of structure and vocabulary. The repetition of words and phrases has been carefully controlled to permit maximum learning of new words without producing a childish effect.

The reading level of the stories was established by the use of the *Fry Readability Formula*. According to this formula, the range of reading levels of the chapters of this book is from grade 1.7 to 2.0.

Eighty-seven percent of the words used in *A City for Ransom* are included in *3,000 Instant Words* by Elizabeth Sakiey and Edward Fry; 80 percent are among the first 2,000 words in that book, which lists the 3,000 most common words in the English language, ranked in order of frequency. The first 100 words on the list and their common variants [-*s*, -*ing*, etc.] make up 50 percent of all written material. The first 300 words and their variants make up 65 percent of all written material. Because readers encounter a relatively small number of words so frequently, they must be able to recognize the Instant Words immediately to be effective readers.

Since *A City for Ransom* is set in the city, some of the concepts presented may be somewhat unfamiliar to students from a more rural environment. These students may profit from an explanation of such topics as city transportation systems, apartment building layout and the job of a building superintendent (or super). This preparation might improve comprehension and enhance the element of reading for pleasure which is the primary purpose of all the stories in the Adult Learner Series.

Structure and Use of the Text

Each book in the Adult Learner Series is divided into several units. Each unit follows a regular format consisting of these sections:

Preview Words

Twenty words from each chapter are presented for students to preview before reading. Those words that were expected to give students the most difficulty were chosen for previewing. The preview section includes all words of more than one syllable that are not among the first 2,000 words on Sakiey and Fry's list of 3,000 Instant Words. The words are listed first in alphabetical order and then shown again in chapter sequence in sentences based on the chapter.

The twenty sentences match the chapter in readability; students can read the sentences independently.

With some classes the instructor may want to read the words and sentences aloud for students to repeat and learn. In very structured classes, the words could also be used for spelling and writing practice.

Story

The primary purpose of the story is to provide interesting material for adult readers. It should be read as a story; the element of pleasure should be present. Because of the second grade reading level, students should be able to read the story on their own.

The first page of each chapter has a gray band at the top. This makes it easy to find the story pages. Students should be encouraged to return to these pages often and to reread the stories.

Comprehension Questions

Ten multiple-choice comprehension questions follow each chapter. There are two questions for each of these five comprehension skills:

A. Recognizing Words in Context
B. Recalling Facts
C. Keeping Events in Order
D. Making Inferences
E. Understanding Main Ideas

The letters *A* through *E* appear in the text as labels to identify the questions.

The comprehension questions are constructed to cover all parts of the chapter evenly and to bring out important points in the story. This insures that the student understands the story so far before going on to the next chapter.

Students should answer the questions immediately after reading the chapter and correct their answers using the key at the back of the book. Students should circle incorrect responses and check off the correct ones.

The graphs at the back of the book help the instructor keep track of each student's comprehension progress. The *Comprehension Progress Graph* shows comprehension percentage scores. The *Skills Profile Graph* identifies areas of comprehension weakness needing special attention and extra practice.

Language Skills

These sections cover many aspects of language study: phonics, word attack skills, simple grammar, and correct usage. The readability of these sections is higher than that of the chapters. The readability level varies depending on the vocabulary load of the specific language skill being taught.

Because the language skills are taught in clear and simple terms, most students will be able to work these sections independently. However, the instructor should be alert for opportunities to explain and further illustrate the content of the lessons.

The lessons contain exercises which give students the opportunity to practice the language skills being taught. An answer key at the back of the book makes it possible for students to correct their work.

Understanding Life Skills

Every chapter is accompanied by two sections which deal with life skills. The first, "Understanding Life Skills," introduces and fully explains a specific life skill. The life skills all revolve around some detail of modern adult life.

Because this section stresses *understanding* a certain life skill, the reading level is higher than the reading level of the story. However, the life skill lessons are presented in carefully prepared steps, and most students should be able to read and comprehend them without too much difficulty.

Questions used in the lessons are designed to focus the students' attention and to reinforce the learning. Answers for all questions are provided at the back of the book.

Applying Life Skills

Because modern-day living requires both *knowing* and *doing*, two life skills sections follow each chapter to emphasize both aspects. The second, "Applying Life Skills," is primarily a practical exercise.

This section builds on the understanding generated in the previous section. Students should be able to complete the exercise successfully by applying what they have just read.

Completing this section allows students to demonstrate their mastery of a specific life skill. It gives them the firsthand experience they need with tasks they are likely to encounter in everyday living.

An Answer Key at the back of the book helps students correct their work and gives them immediate feedback.

All units in each book are structured alike, each consisting of the six sections described here. Students quickly discover the regular pattern and are able to work with success and confidence throughout the text.

Use in Small-Group or Class Situations

Although the books in the Adult Learner Series were designed primarily for use on an individual basis, they can be used successfully in small-group or class situations. The comprehension, language and life skills questions can be adapted to whole-class instruction; this may be especially useful for students of English as a Second Language. If several students have read the stories, a group discussion may prove rewarding as well as motivating.

Writing Assignments

The comprehension questions and answers may also serve as suggestions for writing assignments.

For many students at this level, a writing assignment must be introduced in a very structured manner; otherwise, some students may find themselves unable to get started. On a group basis, the writing assignment may grow naturally out of the class discussion. In this case, the discussion may be all the introduction necessary.

On an individual basis, however, and also often within a group situation, it will be necessary to provide the student with a more concrete starting point. The teacher may find it necessary to provide model sentences or paragraphs, or to supply sentence beginnings ("If I had been there, I would have . . .") for the student to complete. The students can use their copies of the stories to search for word spellings, or the teacher may wish to write suggested words on the blackboard or provide a prepared list.

The Word List

Every word used in the story is included in the Word List, given alphabetically under the chapter in which it is first introduced. New forms that are made by adding the suffixes -s, -ed, -ing, and -ly to words that have already been introduced are indented.

The instructor may wish to scan the Word List to choose preview words in addition to the twenty in the Preview Words section at the beginning of each chapter. Non-phonetic words, which may present some difficulties in decoding, are printed in italics for quick identification.

The Word List may also be used for the study of common sight words. Since an effort has been made to provide adequate repetition of each word, most of these words should be a solid part of the student's sight vocabulary by the time he or she has finished reading the story.

Summary of Chapters in A City for Ransom

Chapter 1: Morning (Level 1.8)

It is morning in the city. Betty Rounds and her two children, Frank and Lynn, are getting ready for the day. Frank, who enjoys spying on the other tenants of the apartment building, reports that some new tenants, three men, have moved in. As they leave their apartment, Betty and the children meet Mrs. Katz, an elderly neighbor, and Mr. Logan, the temporary superintendent of the building.

Chapter 2: Screams in the Dark *(Level 2.0)*

Betty is coming home from work on the subway. In the subway station, she sees one of the new tenants from her building. The train leaves the station, but stops suddenly in the tunnel. Trapped in the dark, the passengers begin to push and shove; they are calmed by the singing of a woman and of a gang of boys. Then someone screams that he smells gas, and people are trampled in the ensuing panic. Betty escapes and runs down the tunnel to the next station. She gets home at last, to find that Mr. Logan has caught Frank taking mail out of his mailbox.

Chapter 3: We're Going Down! *(Level 1.7)*

The next morning, Betty reads in the newspaper that three people had been killed in the subway panic. She takes the bus to work, where everyone is discussing the subway incident. Betty leaves early and picks up Lynn at her day care center to take her to the dentist by bus. As they go over a bridge, a bomb goes off. The bridge buckles, throwing the bus down against the guard rail. The passengers escape just as the bridge buckles farther. When Betty and Lynn get home, they find Frank, Mr. Logan and Mrs. Katz talking. Frank has found out that the new tenants have guns.

Chapter 4: A Box Full of Bombs *(Level 2.0)*

The next morning, Betty wakes up to find that Frank has disappeared. She panics, fearing that the new tenants have kidnapped him, but he has been with Mr. Logan. Betty calls the police about the new tenants, but they tell her they can't spare a cruiser because a bomb has exploded at the airport. Frank says that the new tenants must be behind all this. Mr. Logan suggests that they check out the men's apartment. Mrs. Katz agrees to stand guard, but leaves her post. The men return while Betty is still in their apartment.

Chapter 5: Hostage! *(Level 1.8)*

Betty climbs out the window onto a ledge on the outside of the building. She begins to fall, but grabs the fire escape. The men see her and realize that she has been in their apartment. They get her, Mr. Logan and Mrs. Katz in Mr. Logan's apartment. The men explain that they are gong to hold the city for ransom by crippling the transportation systems. Frank and Lynn throw the men off by getting Mrs. Katz's cats to attack them. One of the men recovers and holds Betty hostage. Frank rescues Betty again and the police pick up the men. The story ends with Betty and Frank, Lynn, Mrs. Katz and Mr. Logan having a dinner party to celebrate their survival.

Words Introduced in the Story

Non-phonetic words are in italics. New forms of words already introduced are indented.

Chapter 1: Morning

a
about
after
again
against
ago
all
almost
alone
already
always
am
an
and
another
any
anyone
anything
apartment
apple
are
aren't
arm
  arms
around
as
asked
at
away

back
backwards
bag
ball
be
bed
  beds
been
believe
below
bet
better
Betty
  Betty's
big
black
blew
block
  blocks
book
  books
both
bottom
box
  boxes
boy
bread
breakfast
breath
bring
broken

brother
Browns
brush
  brushed
building
burned
bus
but
by

called
calm
came
can
can't
care
  cares
careful
cars
cats
center
chairs
children
city
clean
climb
clock
coat
coffee
cold
come

comes
coming
could
couldn't
course
crazy
cup

dangerous
day
  days
dear
did
didn't
dirt
dishes
do
  doing
does
doesn't
done
don't
door
down
dragged
dress
  dressed
drink
drop
  dropped

eat
  eating
egg
eight
else
end
enough

escape
even
ever
every
everything

far
fast
fat
feel
fill
find
fine
fire
fix
  fixed
floor
for
found
four
Frank
  Frank's
Franklin
from
front
full
fun
fuse
Fuzz

gave
get
  gets
  getting
girl
give
go
  going

gone
good
good-bye
got
grabbed
grouch
growled

had
hair
hall
hand
  hands
happen
hard
  hardly
has
hate
have
haven't
he
head
hear
heard
he'd
held
he'll
hello
help
  helped
her
here
herself
he's
himself
his
home
hope

hot
how
hug
  hugged
hurry
  hurried
hurt

I
if
I'll
I'm
in
into
is
it
it's
I've

job
just

Katz
  Katz's
keep
key
kids
kind
kitchen
kittens
know

last
late
law
lean
  leaned
leave

led
let
like
little
live
  lived
locked
Logan
  Logan's
long
look
  looked
  looking
  looks
lot
lunch
  lunches
Lynn
  Lynn's

made
make
  makes
  making
man
Mama
many
maybe
me
meat
men
  men's
mess
milk
mind
minute
missed
Mom

more
morning
mother
  mother's
move
  moved
  moving
mouth
Mr.
Mrs.
much
must
myself

names
need
never
new
next
nice
night
no
noise
not
now

of
off
oh
OK
old
on
one
only
open
  opened
operas
or

other
out
outside
over

peek
  peeking
people
  people's
pick
  picked
piece
place
please
plugged
popped
pot
pull
  pulled
  pulling
punish
put

quick
  quickly
quiet
  quietly
quite

railing
ran
reading
  reads
ready
refrigerator
repair
repairman
rest

right
room
Rounds
running
  runs
rushed

sadly
said
sandwich
  sandwiches
saw
say
  saying
  says
school
second
see
seem
she
she'll
she's
shoes
shouldn't
shouting
shut
sidewalk
  sidewalks
since
sip
sister
  sister's
sitting
sleep
  sleeping
small
smiled
so

soap
sock
softly
some
somehow
someone
something
somewhere
son
soon
sorry
splash
spying
stairs
stomped
stand
  standing
start
  started
  starting
stay
steps
sticking
still
stood
stop
  stopped
store
stove
streets
stuff
subway
suitcases
super

table
  tables
take

taking
talk
  talking
teacher
tell
  telling
thank
that
that's
the
their
them
then
there
there's
these
they
they're
thing
  things
think
third
this
those
thought
three
through
tie
  tied
tightly
till
time
to
today
told
tonight
too
took

train
truck
try
  tried
  trying
turn
  turned
TV
twenty
twenty-four
two

up
used

very

wait
  waiting
walk
want
  wanted
  wants
was
wasn't
watch
  watched
  watches
  watching
water
wave
  waved
way
we
well
we'll
week
weekend

went
were
we're
we've
what
what's
where
where's
when
while
who
why
window
  windows
without
work
would
wouldn't

year
  years
yelled
yes
yet
you
you'll
your
you're
you've

above
ahead
air
alive
along
anyway
 asking

 backs
bang
 being
before
began
behind
bells
Benny
beside
 boy's
 boys
brat
bumped
 bumping
 burning

carry
 carried
 car
 chair
changed
chariot
chest
child
chin
close
 closing
conductor

cook
crew
crowd
 crowds
cry
 crying
cut

danger
dark
darkness
dead
deep
 doors
 dragging
Dukes

each
emergency
 ended
 ends
everyone
everywhere
eye
 eyes

face
fall
fear
feet
fell
felt
few
first
fish
five

flashlight
 flashlights
foot
footsteps
funny

gang
gas
gasped
 gasping
great
green
ground

handle
 happened
 harder
 hated
heavy
hey
hit
hold
 holding
hung

inside
its

jackets
jail
jingle
Jordan
jumped

kept
knew

lady
  later
lead
leg
letter
light
  lights
lit
loaf
louder
  loudly
low

mail
mailbox
Manny
match
mean
meet
mixed
moment

  named
near

  ones
onto
  opening
  openings
  others
ow

pitch
platform
pointed
policemen
poor
purse

push
  pushed
  pushes
  pushing

questions
  quieter

rail
  rails
rat
reached
real
  really
red
ride
roar
  roared
rob
  robbed
Robert
rocked

safe
sang
scared
screamed
  screaming
  screams
  seemed
seen
shining
shopping
should
  shouted
  shouts
sick
side

sing
  singing
six
skin
slid
slowing
  slowly
smell
  soft
song
  sooner
sound
  sounded
  sounds
  splashed
station
  step
  stepped
  stopping
strap
  street
stuck
suddenly
supper
sure
swayed
sweet
swing

tall
thin
  thinking
threw
throw
tiny
tired
tomorrow
toward

trapped
tunnel

walked

under
unlocked
us
  use

voice

walls
weren't
who's
wished
with

woman
  woman's
won't
worried
writing

yesterday

Chapter 3: We're Going Down!

across
aid
anywhere
asleep
ate

bad
bent
bit
boats
bomb
boom
brave
breathe
bridge
  broke
  Brown
buckled
  bump
buzzing

  call
  calling
  carrying
checked
clear
  climbed

closed
closer
cloth
  conductors
crack
crash
  crashed
  crashing
crawl
  crawled
  crawling
crews
cried
crowded

dare
dentist
dizzy
drank
dream
  dreamed
driver
during

early
everything's

families
  feeling
flash
forever
forget
friends

glad
  goes
gun
  guns

happy
  headed
headline
  heads
hour
  hours
huge

jumping

killed
kit
  knows

laid
lap
lay
  leaning
  leaving
  legs
let's
life
lifted
line
  lock
luck
lying

machine
  mailboxes
  man's
might
mile
most

newspaper
  newspapers
newsstand
nothing

paid
pain
paper
part
past

picking
pieces
pile
  policeman

read
remember
river
road
rolled
rumble
  rumbled
  rush

sat
scraped
  scraping
seat
  seats
set
sewing
shook
  shop
  shout
silly
  sit
slide
  sliding
  smaller
sometime
spinning

spot
stared
  stayed
story
such
  suitcase

teeth
thousands
  tight
tipped
top
touched
towers
  trains
treat
trip
  trucks
  turning
twisted
  tying

upset
uptown

  walking
wall
wide
woke
worked

Chapter 4: A Box Full of Bombs

address
airport
  ask

bags
banged
banging
because

bedroom
best
  bombs
busy

call
calls
cat
cereal
change
check
cleaned
clothes

doorbell
doorway
dove
downstairs

faster
filling
fixing

groups

hanging
heart
he's
hid
hide
hungry

isn't
itself

keys
kid
kitty

knowing

left
lift
living
lots

main
maps
middle
mine
minutes

name

our
own

pat
peekhole
phone
pipe
pipes
plan
plans
planes
police
police's
pounded
pounding
problem
problems
putting

rang
robe
rolls

Saturday
seems
send
sleepy
sleepily
sneak
spoon
staring
surprise

take
thanks
they've
TNT

unless
unlocking
unroll
upstairs

wake
wildly
will
wire
worry
wow

yourself

Chapter 5: Hostage!

afraid
animals

basement
Blackie
blow
  boomed
break
  breathing
  bringing
broadcast

  cans
chance
clang
clawing
  claws
  crowding
  cutting

dinner
dollars
  drive

ear

  facing
  falling
fence
fist
flat
flew
food
froze
  frozen

garbage
grinning

handcuffs
  happily
heap
  heavily
hostage
  hostages

inch
  inches

  kill
knock

land
  landed
Larry
ledge
  lined
lose
loudspeaker

matter
  messing
million
  millions
money
murdered
  murderers

narrow
neck
neckties
note

once
our
  ours

parked
party
pockets
  pointing
policewoman
post

radio
ransom
rattled
  reach
  reaching
rid
  round
rubbed
  rubbing

save
  seeing
sell
shaking
sharp
shoot
shot
sky
slam
  slammed
slipped
snapped
spike
  spikes
splat

spun
  stores
stumbled
  subways
  surprised
swung

taste
  things
thrown
trick

voices

warning

yell
yelling
you'd

Answer Key

Answer Key

Comprehension Questions

Chapter 1
1. b	2. a	3. d	4. a	5. c
6. b	7. d	8. a	9. c	10. c

Chapter 2
1. c	2. c	3. d	4. c	5. b
6. a	7. c	8. d	9. b	10. a

Chapter 3
1. d	2. b	3. c	4. b	5. c
6. a	7. d	8. d	9. c	10. d

Chapter 4
1. c	2. a	3. a	4. b	5. b
6. c	7. d	8. b	9. c	10. c

Chapter 5
1. b	2. d	3. a	4. c	5. b
6. d	7. c	8. a	9. b	10. d

Language Skills

Chapter 1: Exercise 1

1. Sue
2. book
3. man
4. Ellen
5. cookies
6. They
7. truck
8. chair
9. flower
10. We
11. Ted
12. sky

Exercise 2

1. dog
2. car
3. shirt
4. bag
5. I
6. We
7. Frank
8. Lisa
9. window
10. night
11. aunt
12. man

Chapter 2: Exercise 1

1. hit
2. plays
3. reads
4. carries
5. runs
6. moved
7. blew
8. drives
9. work
10. holds
11. swings
12. stole

Exercise 2

1. hit
2. see
3. hears
4. push
5. jumps
6. cuts
7. pulls
8. sit
9. go
10. come
11. throws
12. crosses

Chapter 3: Exercise 1

1. pans	P	pan	S
2. radio	S	radios	P
3. tables	P	table	S
4. shirt	S	shirts	P
5. keys	P	key	S
6. fence	S	fences	P

Exercise 2

1. beach
   singular

2. clouds
   plural

3. bridge
   singular

4. John
   singular

5. apples
   plural

6. newspapers
   plural

7. sheets
   plural

Exercise 3

1. paint
2. write
3. spill
4. explore

5. answer
6. rest
7. listen

Exercise 4

1. fight
   plural

2. hangs
   singular

3. gives
   singular

4. stops
   singular

5. change
   plural

6. slashes
   singular

7. cooks
   singular

Chapter 4: Exercise 1

1. talks   Mary talks.
2. plays   The baby plays.
3. cleans   The man cleans.
4. turns   Jack turns.
5. bends   The flower bends.
6. cuts   The knife cuts.
7. sleeps   The cat sleeps.
8. shines   The sun shines.
9. breaks   The chair breaks.
10. opens   The door opens.
11. rings   The bell rings.
12. stands   The woman stands.

Exercise 2

1. eats
2. lifts
3. builds

4. slides
5. covers
6. smiles

7. puts
8. buys
9. brings

10. feels
11. rocks
12. sharpens

Chapter 5: Exercise 1

1. look — The children look.
2. stop — The trains stop.
3. listen — The sisters listen.
4. run — The dogs run.
5. swim — The ducks swim.
6. wave — The boys wave.
7. sag — The beds sag.
8. fall — The leaves fall.
9. grow — The plants grow.
10. rise — The airplanes rise.

Exercise 2

1. make
2. smell
3. taste
4. dial
5. sweep

6. cut
7. answer
8. arrive
9. tick
10. ring

Exercise 3

1. hold
2. hears
3. hide
4. stays
5. closes

6. give
7. scrape
8. writes
9. smell
10. jumps

Understanding Life Skills

Chapter 1

1. BOOKKEEPER
2. BOOKKEEPER
3. MECHANIC

Chapter 2

1. BARTENDER
2. No
3. a. No
   b. No
4. Will train.
5. a. Thomson Tool Co.
   b. Personnel Office

Chapter 3

1. MAINTENANCE PERSON
2. No
3. 100 pounds

Chapter 4

1. mechanic
2. Edwards
3. Syracuse
4. 3
5. Yes

Chapter 5

1. mechanic
2. By the week
3. moved
4. one

Applying Life Skills

Chapter 1: Exercise 1

1. REPAIR PERSON
2. SALAD BAR ATTENDANT
3. TIRE CHANGER
4. TYPIST

Exercise 2

1. SALAD BAR ATTENDANT
2. TYPIST
3. TIRE CHANGER
4. REPAIR PERSON

Exercise 3

(Answers may be in any order.)

BAKER'S ASSISTANT
COOK'S HELPER

Chapter 2

1. a. evenings
   b. telephone
   c. week
   d. excellent

2. a. $250 per week
   b. Benefits excellent
   c. Part-time evenings
   d. Beginning position
   e. Call Mrs. Jones

Chapter 3: Exercise 1

1. a. over 21
    b. used to handling money
    c. able to do business on the phone

Exercise 2

1. a. Yes
    b. Yes
    c. Yes

Exercise 3

1. a. 24 years old
    b. cashier
    c. has taken phone orders

Chapter 4

APPLICATION FOR EMPLOYMENT

POSITION DESIRED _Switchboard operator_

PERSONAL INFORMATION

DATE Month _July_ Day _1,_ Year _1993_ **SOCIAL SECURITY NUMBER** _272 - 50 - 8253_

NAME Last _Biggs_ First _Sarah_ Middle Initial _A._

ADDRESS Street _944 Wood Ave._ City _Akron,_ State _Ohio_ Zip _45126_

PHONE _782 - 5946_ **NUMBER OF DEPENDENTS** _1_ **MARITAL STATUS** (check one) Single ☑ Married ☐ Divorced ☐

U.S. CITIZEN (check one) Yes ☑ No ☐ **DATE OF BIRTH** Month _February 20,_ Day Year _1957_

Chapter 5

EMPLOYMENT RECORD (List last three employers, starting with last one first.)

DATE Month Year	NAME AND ADDRESS OF EMPLOYER	PHONE	POSITION	PAY	REASON FOR LEAVING
From *March 1985* To *Present*	*Manson Company 86 Lake Drive Akron, Ohio 45120*	*487-6400*	*Switch-board operator*	*$350 per Week*	*moved*
From *March 1980* To *March 1985*	*Chase and Sons 95 Vine St. Akron, Ohio 45122*	*396-5430*	*Switch-board operator*	*$300 per week*	*Poor benefits*
From To					

REFERENCES

NAME	ADDRESS	PHONE	JOB TITLE AND EMPLOYER
Ms. Jane Anders	95 Vine Street Akron, Ohio 45122	396-5430	Supervisor Chase and Sons
Ms. Martha Mc Hughes	95 Vine Street Akron, Ohio 45122	396-5430	Personnel Director Chase and Sons
Mr. Peter Hutton	86 Lake Drive Akron, Ohio 45120	487-6400	Personnel Manager Manson Company

DATE July 1, 1993   SIGNATURE Sarah A. Biggs

Comprehension Progress Graph
Skills Profile Graph

Comprehension Progress Graph

How to Use the Comprehension Progress Graph

1. At the top of the graph, find the number of the chapter you have just read.
2. Follow the line down until it crosses the line for the number of questions you got right.
3. Put a dot • where the lines cross.
4. The numbers on the other side of the graph show your comprehension score.

For example, this graph shows the score of a student who answered 7 questions right for Chapter 1. The score is 70%. →

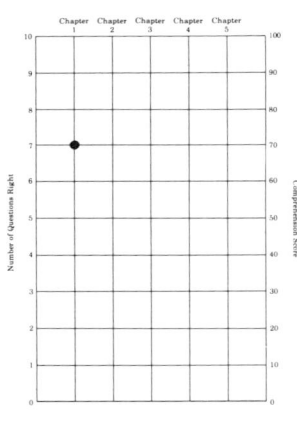

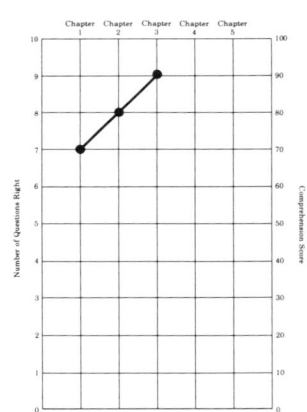

This same student got scores of 80% and 90% on Chapters 2 and 3. The line connecting ← the dots keeps going up. This shows that the student is doing well.

If the line between the dots on your graph does not go up, or if it goes down, see your instructor for help.

Comprehension Progress

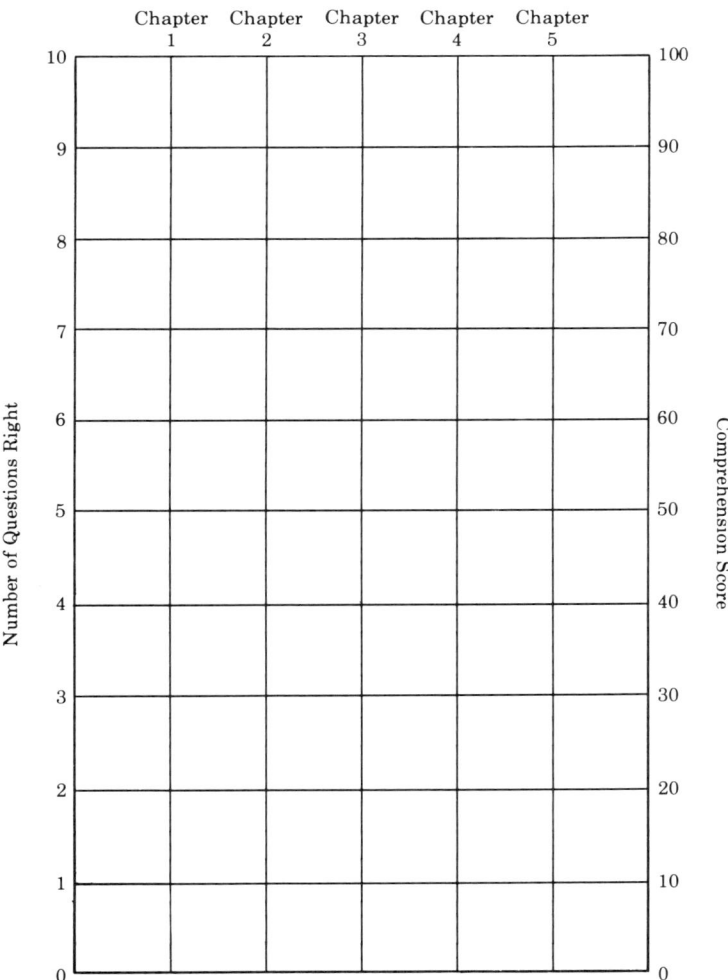

Skills Profile Graph

How to Use the Skills Profile Graph

1. There is a block on this graph for every comprehension question in the book.
2. Every time you get a question wrong, fill in a block which has the same letter as the question you got wrong. For example, if you get an A question wrong, fill in a block in the A row. Use the right row for each letter.

Look at the graph. It shows the profile of a student who got 3 questions wrong. This student got an A question wrong, a C question wrong, and a D question wrong.

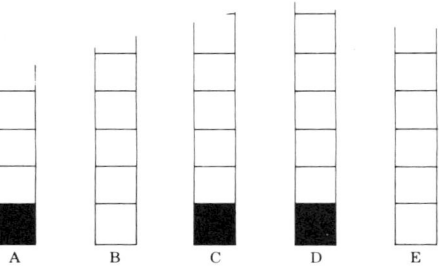

On the next chapter, this same student got 4 questions wrong and has filled in 4 more blocks.

The graph now looks like this. This student seems to be having trouble on question C. This shows a reading skill that needs to be worked on.

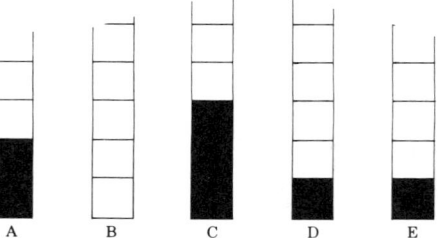

The blocks that are filled in on your graph tell you and your instructor the kinds of questions that give you trouble.

Look for the rows that have the most blocks filled in. These rows will be higher than the others. Talk to your instructor about them. Your instructor may want to give you extra help on these skills.

Skills Profile

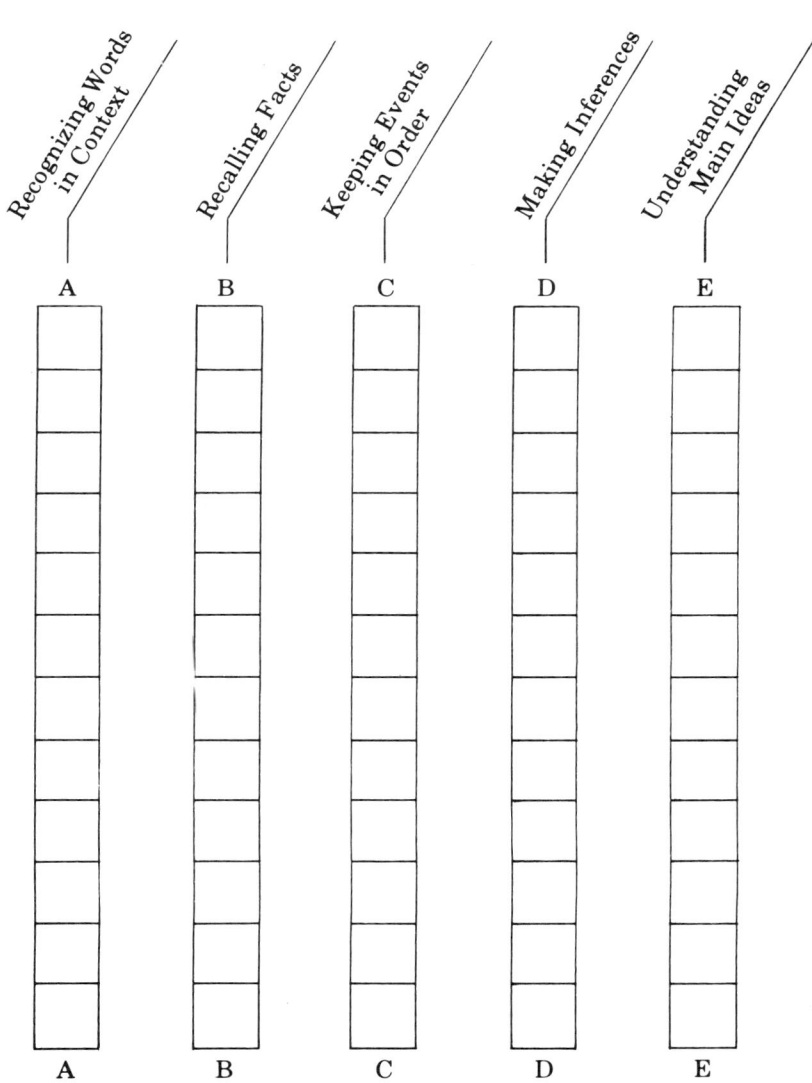